Ralph G. Brockett, *University of Tennessee, Knoxville*
EDITOR-IN-CHIEF

Alan B. Knox, *University of Wisconsin, Madison*
CONSULTING EDITOR

Overcoming Resistance to Self-Direction in Adult Learning

Roger Hiemstra
Syracuse University

Ralph G. Brockett
University of Tennesee, Knoxville

EDITORS

Number 64, Winter 1994

JOSSEY-BASS PUBLISHERS
San Francisco

OVERCOMING RESISTANCE TO SELF-DIRECTION IN ADULT LEARNING
Roger Hiemstra, Ralph G. Brockett (eds.)
New Directions for Adult and Continuing Education, no. 64
Ralph G. Brockett, Editor-in-Chief
Alan B. Knox, Consulting Editor

Microfilm copies of issues and articles are available in 16mm and 35mm, as well as microfiche in 105mm, through University Microfilms Inc., 300 North Zeeb Road, Ann Arbor, Michigan 48106-1346.

LC 85-644750   ISSN 0195-2242   ISBN 0-7879-9981-4

NEW DIRECTIONS FOR ADULT AND CONTINUING EDUCATION is part of The Jossey-Bass Higher and Adult Education Series and is published quarterly by Jossey-Bass Inc., Publishers, 350 Sansome Street, San Francisco, California 94104-1342 (publication number USPS 493-930). Second-class postage paid at San Francisco, California, and at additional mailing offices. POSTMASTER: Send address changes to New Directions for Adult and Continuing Education, Jossey-Bass Inc., Publishers, 350 Sansome Street, San Francisco, California 94104-1342.

SUBSCRIPTIONS for 1994 cost $47.00 for individuals and $62.00 for institutions, agencies, and libraries.

EDITORIAL CORRESPONDENCE should be sent to the Editor-in-Chief, Ralph G. Brockett, Department of Educational Leadership, University of Tennessee, 239 Claxton Addition, Knoxville, Tennessee 37996-3400.

Cover photograph by Wernher Krutein/PHOTOVAULT © 1990.

Manufactured in the United States of America. Nearly all Jossey-Bass books, jackets, and periodicals are printed on recycled paper that contains at least 50 percent recycled waste, including 10 percent postconsumer waste. Many of our materials are also printed with vegetable-based inks; during the printing process, these inks emit fewer volatile organic compounds (VOCs) than petroleum-based inks. VOCs contribute to the formation of smog.

CONTENTS

EDITORS' NOTES

One of the most important influences in recent years on successful practice in adult education is the idea of self-direction in adult learning. Over the past twenty-five years, few topics have received as much attention, been studied as extensively, or generated more controversy than self-direction. In a previous book, we reviewed much of the theory, research, and practice related to self-direction (Brockett and Hiemstra, 1991).

At that time, we defined self-direction as "both the external characteristics of an instructional process and the internal characteristics of the learner, where the individual assumes primary responsibility for a learning experience" (p. 24). To clarify this distinction, we developed the Personal Responsibility Orientation (PRO) model.

Central to the PRO model is a distinction between *self-directed learning,* the external characteristics of the teaching and learning process, and *learner self-direction,* the individual's internal characteristics. We felt it important to distinguish between the instructional process side and the personal orientation or individual side. The interaction between these two makes up the broader concept that we have called *self-direction in learning.*

An important aspect of the PRO model is its view of the individual as the starting point for understanding self-direction. At the same time the model describes a need to understand the social context in which learning takes place. Some authors (for example, Candy, 1991; Brookfield, 1993) believe that social context should be the starting point for understanding self-direction. Indeed, the PRO model has been challenged (Flannery, 1993) because of its emphasis on the individual. While we argue that notions about individuals are central to the PRO model, we also believe it impossible to truly understand all dimensions of self-direction without recognizing the importance of social and cultural contexts. This also ties to our acceptance of humanism as a strong underlying philosophy for self-direction in learning (Hiemstra and Brockett, 1994). We welcome criticism and intellectual exchange because they clarify, complement, and expand thinking about the model and definitions of self-direction.

Much is known about both self-directed learning and learner self-direction. However, the literature appears to show considerable confusion between these two dimensions. For example, relatively little is known about how these two dimensions are linked. We believe that the idea of personal responsibility offers a key to understanding such linkage. To us, personal responsibility means that individuals assume ownership for their own thoughts and actions. They may not always have control of all their life circumstances, but they do have the potential to direct how they respond to any situation.

Another result of the confusion between these two dimensions is a tendency for both teachers and learners to intermingle associated ideas or practices without critical thought about potential differences. For example, some teachers assume that all learners will readily accept the learning-contract approach to planning and implementing learning activities. On the other hand, some learners will have unrealistic expectations about a teacher's ability to allow them complete freedom of choice. Such misunderstandings or unrealistic expectations lead to resistance to self-direction.

To give another example, it is not unusual to hear teachers of adults suggest that while self-direction is a "nice idea" that "works in theory," it does not fit their situation because they have content that must be taught in a certain way or because their subject matter is mandated. Learners, too, sometimes have initial hesitancy in accepting that they are self-directed or can take personal ownership because of self-doubts about learning abilities or because of constraints placed on them by teachers and organizations.

This concept of personal ownership, or what some refer to as empowerment (Hiemstra and Sisco, 1990; Orsburn, Moran, Musselwhite, and Zenger, 1990; Piskurich, 1993), can be thought of as the personal values we attach to making decisions, taking control, or accepting responsibility for our beliefs and actions. We believe such personal values are measurable, as they vary from one person to the next. However, we know of no research that identifies valid measures for assessing such values; this is an obvious area for future study, dialogue, and publications.

The purpose of this volume is to describe various instances where resistance to self-direction has been overcome and where individuals have been helped to accept increasing responsibility for their own learning. It is also intended to help readers understand some of the sources of resistance and become better able to identify strategies that enable educators and trainers of adults to overcome such resistance. The volume brings together a nice mixture of people carrying out research related to self-direction in learning and people who are testing out related notions with various audiences and in various settings.

In Chapter One, Ralph G. Brockett provides a framework for the volume by exploring several myths and misunderstandings that can contribute to resistance. This chapter suggests that it is important to understand what self-direction is and what it is not. Further, it points out that an understanding of myths can help adult and continuing educators work toward overcoming sources of resistance within their organizational settings and in their own practice.

Huey B. Long, in Chapter Two, provides a bridge to the remainder of the volume by presenting a discussion of key terms, major sources of resistance, and strategies for overcoming resistance. In addition, he examines a wide range of resources from the literature related to resistance and self-direction in learning. These resources may be helpful to readers who wish to look beyond this volume for information and ideas about resistance to self-direction.

Jean Ellen Jones, in Chapter Three, examines portfolio assessment as a particular strategy or approach for promoting self-direction in the formal classroom setting. She uses art education examples to demonstrate how portfolios have been successfully used to overcome resistance both for teachers and for learners.

In Chapter Four, Gary J. Confessore and Sharon J. Confessore describe how self-direction has been utilized in the continuing education of two professional groups, physicians and architects. The authors address the nature of professions and the importance of reflective practice. From this framework, they describe sources of resistance to self-direction in continuing professional education and strategies that can be used to address the problem within this context.

Business and industry provides an ideal context for applying principles of self-direction. However, as Lucy M. Guglielmino and Paul J. Guglielmino point out in Chapter Five, this context also is ripe for many sources of resistance. By describing examples of successfully implemented self-direction efforts, they provide a framework for understanding how such resistance can be overcome.

Constance C. Blackwood, in Chapter Six, discusses the potentials and pitfalls of self-direction in a technical training setting where participation is mandated. While mandatory continuing education is incompatible with many of the basic tenets of self-direction, she discusses ways to break down resistance to mandatory learning approaches.

In Chapter Seven, Thomas D. Phelan describes how various technology-based innovations have been used to promote a self-directed approach to career development among employees in a power utility. He outlines a five-step process that presents several study choices to individuals and details how technology has helped many to overcome resistance to self-direction in learning.

There has been much controversy about the appropriateness of measuring self-direction in learners. Jane Pilling-Cormick has recently developed a new instrument to measure perceptions of self-directedness. In Chapter Eight she describes her experiences with instructors who were reluctant to use the instrument in their classes. She discusses possible reasons for and solutions to this kind of dilemma.

Susan B. Slusarski, in Chapter Nine, describes a variety of techniques that can be used to overcome resistance to self-direction in learning both by learners and by teachers. Such techniques as helping learners increase their technical learning skills, become more familiar with subject matter, and enhance their personal learning competence are examined.

In Chapter Ten, Roger Hiemstra describes a framework of seventy-eight microcomponents of the teaching and learning process that provides learners with various opportunities to take increased responsibility for study efforts. The chapter includes a checklist detailing each component and provides suggestions on how the checklist can be utilized to overcome resistance to undertaking self-directed learning.

Self-direction has been a major source of discussion for nearly twenty-five years. While there has been much research, debate, and dialogue about this topic, there remain many unanswered questions. Chapter Eleven, by Roger Hiemstra and Ralph G. Brockett, summarizes key concepts from the prior chapters on overcoming resistance to self-direction in learning. They also detail some of the future study needed to address the various unanswered questions. Thus, this volume has been developed as a means for moving the dialogue on self-direction into some uncharted territory. This final chapter should provide a springboard for such reflection and discussion.

Roger Hiemstra
Ralph G. Brockett
Editors

References

Brockett, R. G., and Hiemstra, R. *Self-Direction in Adult Learning: Perspectives on Theory, Research, and Practice.* New York: Routledge & Kegan Paul, 1991.

Brookfield, S. D. "Self-Directed Learning, Political Clarity, and the Critical Practice of Adult Education." *Adult Education Quarterly,* 1993, 43 (4), 227–242.

Candy, P. C. *Self-Direction for Lifelong Learning: A Comprehensive Guide to Theory and Practice.* San Francisco: Jossey-Bass, 1991.

Flannery, D. D. Review of *Self-Direction in Adult Learning. Adult Education Quarterly,* 1993, 43 (2), 110–112.

Hiemstra, R., and Brockett, R. G. "From Behaviorism to Humanism: Incorporating Self-Direction in Learning Concepts into the Instructional Design Process." In H. B. Long and Associates, *New Ideas About Self-Directed Learning.* Norman: Oklahoma Research Center for Continuing Professional and Higher Education, University of Oklahoma, 1994.

Hiemstra, R., and Sisco, B. *Individualizing Instruction: Making Learning Personal, Empowering, and Successful.* San Francisco: Jossey-Bass, 1990.

Orsburn, J. D., Moran, L., Musselwhite, E., and Zenger, J. H. *Self-Directed Work Teams: The New American Challenge.* Homewood, Ill.: Business One Irwin, 1990.

Piskurich, G. M. *Self-Directed Learning: A Practical Guide to Design, Development, and Implementation.* San Francisco: Jossey-Bass, 1993.

ROGER HIEMSTRA is professor of instructional design and adult learning, Syracuse University. He has carried out scholarship related to self-direction in learning for twenty years.

RALPH G. BROCKETT is associate professor of adult education in the Leadership Studies Unit, University of Tennessee, Knoxville. He has been involved with self-direction in learning scholarship for fifteen years and is editor-in-chief of New Directions for Adult and Continuing Education.

Resistance often results from a lack of understanding about self-direction in learning.

Resistance to Self-Direction in Adult Learning: Myths and Misunderstandings

Ralph G. Brockett

For more than a quarter of a century, the notion of self-direction in learning has been at the center of discussions about the study and practice of adult and continuing education. Regardless of whether one chooses to trace the origins of this emphasis to Houle's (1961) *The Inquiring Mind,* Johnstone and Rivera's (1965) *Volunteers for Learning,* Knowles's (1968, 1970) early discussions of andragogy, or Tough's (1979) study of adults' learning projects (originally published in 1971), it should be clear by now that self-direction is no longer a "new idea," "current trend," "passing fad," or "hot topic." Instead, it is an idea that has helped to transform the way a great many educators of adults approach their practice. Elsewhere, Hiemstra and I have attempted to outline major developments in theory, research, and practice relative to self-direction (Brockett and Hiemstra, 1991).

However, as most educators recognize, change rarely comes easily. Over more than a decade and a half, I have had the opportunity to study the concept of self-direction and to implement principles of self-direction in a great many practice settings, ranging from graduate and undergraduate classrooms to continuing professional education workshops and training programs. While the vast majority of my experiences with self-direction have been positive and enriching both for the learners and for me, I frequently find myself responding to questions and challenges about the relevance or desirability of turning over responsibility to learners.

Frequently, resistance to self-direction can be traced to misinformation about the nature and practice of self-direction. One way in which this has often happened is with regard to the link between self-direction and humanism. The purpose of this chapter, therefore, is to focus on some of the myths and misunderstandings that can promote resistance to self-direction in adult learning. Specifically, I will review ten common myths about self-direction, with special attention to the way each myth can lead to resistance. I will then focus on some common misunderstandings about humanism and self-direction and how these can also contribute to resistance.

Revisiting Some Common Myths About Self-Direction in Adult Learning

Previously, Hiemstra and I identified ten myths frequently associated with self-direction (Brockett and Hiemstra, 1991). Our original intent was to discuss some of the misconceptions that have led to confusion over the meaning of self-direction and its implementation in practice. In reviewing these myths, it is clear that each has implications for promoting resistance from learners, facilitators, and institutions. Therefore, it makes sense to reexamine these myths with specific emphasis on how each can contribute to increased resistance to self-direction.

Myth 1: Self-directedness is an all-or-nothing concept. It is not uncommon to hear educators speak of self-direction as a dichotomous or either/or concept. In this view, a learning situation is viewed as either self-directed or instructor directed and the learner is seen is being either self-directed or not self-directed. By breaking down self-direction into either/or terms, it is easy to identify a major source of resistance. Such a view ignores that (1) learners vary greatly in learning style and, thus, will likely possess different degrees of self-directedness, and (2) educators or trainers vary greatly in teaching style and, thus, will promote different degrees of self-direction in their instructional settings. When self-direction is viewed as an all-or-nothing concept, it can become easy to place labels on learners who are not self-directed and instructors who do not promote self-directed learning.

A different approach is to think about self-direction as a continuum where it "is viewed as a characteristic that exists, to a greater or lesser degree, in all persons and in all learning situations" (Brockett and Hiemstra, 1991, p. 11). The advantage of this view is that it recognizes a vast range where learners and learning situations are found to be more or less self-directed.

In terms of overcoming resistance, this approach makes it possible for instructors, particularly those who prefer or are required to use a highly prescriptive approach, to incorporate elements of self-direction into the teaching-learning process. It also means that self-direction can be a goal toward which learners can strive rather than a label that can erroneously be used to rate their success as learners. In Chapter Ten of this volume, Hiemstra identifies seventy-eight "microcomponents" that allow instructors or learners to incorporate elements of self-direction into their practice. Thus, a trainer in a nuclear power facility might be required to teach highly prescribed content and to use a standard evaluation form in a safety training workshop, but there may be aspects of the program, such as pacing the learning or controlling the learning environment, where the trainer may be able to turn over varying degrees of control. When viewed in this way, self-direction can be seen as a process rather than an outcome.

Myth 2: Self-direction implies learning in isolation. A frequent stereotype of the self-directed learner is of a person who works in isolation and does not share the fruits of the learning with others. It is not surprising to realize that such a myth could easily lead educators and trainers in institutional settings to resist promoting such an approach. Most of us recognize the joy and synergy that results from interacting with others in our learning efforts; learning in isolation clearly conflicts with this approach.

However, the idea that most self-directed learning situations isolate the students is a myth. It is true that such situations are often characterized by times of intense, focused individual inquiry. Yet, at some point, interaction is what makes new insights and growth possible. Take writing, for example. As I write these words, it is early morning and I am working alone in my study. I am able to turn inward and gain insights that I can share on these pages. But for me, the real potential for growth from this experience will come in interactions with my coeditor and with colleagues in the field who read and respond to the ideas presented. It is these interactions that will give life to the somewhat abstract ideas that appear in print.

While success in self-directed learning often requires that learners have ample time to be alone for personal reflection, reading, and writing, this is only one aspect of the learning process. Educators who seek to break down resistance to self-direction can do so by finding an appropriate balance between individual and group learning activities.

Myth 3: Self-direction is just another adult education fad. As was mentioned above, self-direction in learning has been a major topic in the literature of the adult and continuing education field for about three decades. This is hardly indicative of a fad. Yet it is true that because self-direction has gained widespread use throughout the field, there is the potential for misunderstanding and misappropriation of the term.

In a recent book entitled *Self-Directed Learning: A Practical Guide to Design, Development, and Implementation,* Piskurich (1993) defines self-directed learning as "a training design in which trainees master packages of predetermined material, at their own pace, without the aid of an instructor" (p. 4). He then goes on to describe a systematic instructional design process that resembles a traditional systems analysis procedure. While this book contains many useful strategies, particularly with regard to learning in the workplace, it can be argued that "self-directed learning" is not what Piskurich is addressing because his approach really does little more than give learners control over the pace of their learning. To be sure, learning pace is one component of self-direction, but I contend that the above definition has very little to do with the concept of self-directed learning (or self-direction in learning) that has been the object of three decades of theory, research, and practice. The problem then is that it is possible for educators to adopt this view in an uncritical fashion, without considering the extensive body of knowledge in this area, and be led to think that they are promoting self-direction. This is when self-direction has the potential to be viewed as a fad.

Myth 4: Self-direction is not worth the time required to make it work. This is largely a question of cost-benefit analysis. It is true that most self-directed learning situations require a certain amount of start-up time in order to introduce the process and help learners diagnose their needs, assess possible options for the learning process, negotiate decisions about content and outcomes, and determine how learning will be evaluated. At the same time, because such process activities are directly tied to the learning endeavor, they serve as a way of helping learners move into the learning activity in a smooth manner. Educators and trainers who express resistance to self-direction on the grounds that time spent on process activities detracts from content time are missing the point that the payoff for process activities is likely to be greater communication between learners and facilitator, and ultimately, more efficiency in learning.

Myth 5: Self-directed learning activities are limited primarily to reading and writing. So much of what has been studied and written about self-direction has focused upon learning in formal institutional settings that this myth is not at all surprising. However, such a view fails to recognize the wide array of situations where learning is linked to skill development and performance. Learning how to play a musical instrument, how to make a wood table, how to play tennis, and how to fly an airplane are only four examples where successful learning cannot be achieved solely or primarily from reading and writing. Self-direction holds much promise for skill and performance-based learning because it stresses an experiential approach to learning, where the learner is an active participant rather than a passive recipient of information.

Myth 6: Facilitating self-direction is an easy way out for teachers. Perhaps one of the most pervasive myths regarding self-direction is that it provides an "easy way out" for instructors who are either unprepared or uninterested in working actively with their learners. Those who subscribe to this myth are likely to equate self-direction with a learning environment characterized by a lazy instructor or an anarchic classroom. However, those who work with principles and practices of self-directed learning clearly understand that they need to take a very active approach to working with learners. In fact, self-direction typically involves a deeper commitment from instructors because they need to focus their energy on each learner, as well as on the group as a whole. Hiemstra (1988) has described this teaching-learning transaction in self-directed learning situations as a "learning partnership."

Myth 7: Self-directed learning is limited primarily to those settings where freedom and democracy prevail. Most discussions of self-direction focus on situations where the learner consciously chooses to engage in a learning project, and to do so in a self-directed way. But what about those situations where decisions about participation, content, and process lie outside of the individual? There are many situations where adults are required to participate in a learning activity for a variety of reasons. Examples include the registered nurse who must attend a certain number of continuing education programs in order to maintain certification, the nuclear power plant employee who must attend workshops on nuclear safety, and the adult who is required by the state to attend adult basic education classes in order to continue receiving public assistance.

While the circumstances that bring such learners to the learning activity are antithetical to the spirit of self-direction, it is inaccurate to suggest that there is no place for principles and practices of self-direction in such situations. As Hiemstra discusses in Chapter Ten, the advantage of using the microcomponents approach is that it allows facilitators to incorporate elements of self-direction into situations where many key decisions, including specific content, are predetermined. The point here is that it is possible, even in highly structured learning situations, to move toward self-direction by making sure that the learners have control over as many elements of the process as possible. From this viewpoint, it can be argued that self-direction can, in and of itself, be viewed as a potential strategy for helping facilitators work with learners who may be resistant because of resentment toward the circumstances that led them to the learning activity.

Myth 8: Self-direction in learning is limited primarily to white, middle-class adults. A criticism that is sometimes leveled at self-direction in learning is that it is merely a reflection of mainstream values in our society, and thus has little to offer learners who have traditionally been marginalized or disempowered, such as women and minorities. However, there is an extensive body of research showing that self-direction in learning is a phenomenon that can be found in all strata of our society as well as in many societies outside of North America and western Europe. Indeed, I have been convinced for more than a decade that self-direction holds tremendous potential for reaching those who have been traditionally labeled "hard-to-reach" adults. Its great advantage is that it provides a different approach for working with learners who have rejected more traditional approaches to education due to such factors as rejection, frustration, or boredom (see, for example, Brockett, 1983).

Myth 9: Self-directed learning will erode the quality of institutional programs. According to this view, turning greater responsibility for the learning process over to learners is analogous to letting go of control over quality of programs. To be sure, self-direction principles can be misused in a way that will in fact compromise program quality. However, it is not self-direction itself that raises quality issues; quality declines only when self-direction is improperly implemented. Again, there is an ample body of research and practice literature that addresses ways to successfully incorporate self-direction into various learning settings. Institutions that view their involvement with learners as a partnership should find it quite manageable to incorporate principles and practices of self-directed learning and learner self-direction into their mission and actual practice.

Myth 10: Self-directed learning is the best approach for adults. A final myth that can lead to resistance toward self-direction is one that can actually be promoted by those who actively advocate self-direction, but do so in an uncritical way. In their enthusiasm to embrace an approach that clearly holds much promise, some educators may take the extreme position that self-direction is the best, indeed, the only effective way for adults to learn. This is simply not so! As educators of adults, we need to recognize the vast array of approaches and philosophies available to work successfully with adult learners and to recognize the inherent limitations of any approach. To advocate self-direction as the single best theory, method, or approach to adult learning is to ignore differences in learning styles, teaching styles, and institutional policies. Presenting self-direction as a panacea is clearly a way to promote resistance among those who might otherwise be open to incorporating elements of the approach into their practice.

Misunderstandings About Self-Direction and Humanism

It is important to recognize that there is no single "correct" way to think about self-direction. As an example, three recent books on self-direction in adult learning are written from different points of view. Candy (1991) discusses self-direction from the framework of constructivist sociology. Piskurich (1993) has used behaviorism and instructional systems design to frame his discussion. And Hiemstra and I have drawn largely from the perspective of humanism in our work on self-direction (Brockett and Hiemstra, 1991).

As with any set of principles or practices, educators who wish to promote self-direction in adult learning need to have a basic set of assumptions to guide how they view the concept. My purpose in this chapter is not especially aimed at comparing the relative merits of constructivism, behaviorism, and humanism. Rather, I would like to focus on humanism in terms of the way it can help us to understand self-direction and the way misunderstandings of humanism can contribute to resistance to self-direction.

Humanism has been defined as "a philosophy of joyous service for the greater good of all humanity" (Lamont, 1965, p. 12). According to Elias and Merriam (1980), humanism is rooted in the idea that "human beings are capable of making significant personal choices within the constraints imposed by heredity, personal history, and environment" (p. 118). The basic tenets of humanism hold that human nature is inherently good and that human potential for growth and development is virtually unlimited. In addition, humanism maintains that individuals are free and autonomous, but also have responsibility both to themselves and to others.

It is not difficult to see the compatibility of these ideas with the notion of self-direction. Yet the humanist framework is often subject to challenge. These challenges, which come from both the far right and the far left, can serve to create resistance to self-direction because they aim to discredit key elements of humanism. I would like to address three such criticisms.

First, because humanism stresses the "here and now" and denies existence of the supernatural, it runs contrary to many tenets of Christian and other theological orientations. Indeed, this view is supported by Lamont (1965), who noted that individuals "have but one life to lead and should make the most of it in terms of creative work and happiness" (p. 14). In my fifteen years of experience with self-direction, I have worked successfully with learners from many different religious backgrounds. Bearing in mind that self-direction is not an all-or-nothing concept, I emphasize to learners that one does not have to abandon one's religious beliefs in order to celebrate the good of humanity and to promote self-direction in learning.

Second, some critics have argued that humanism is overly self-centered and excludes concern for the social context of learning and issues of social justice. This is perhaps one of the greatest misunderstandings about humanism. While individual growth is typically the starting point in humanism, there is a clear concern for serving the good of all humanity, as reflected above in our definition of humanism. As an example, O'Hara (1989) has presented a comparison of the ideas of humanist psychologist Carl Rogers and "radical" educator Paulo Freire. According to O'Hara, while the backgrounds and practice of Rogers and Freire differ greatly, the basic values held by the two men are very similar in that both "unabashedly celebrate human existence and our evolutionary potential" and that neither man "gives up on people" (p. 13). Still another example can be found in the following statement by Eduard Lindeman in *The Meaning of Adult Education*: "Adult education will become an agency of progress if its short-time goal of self-improvement can be made compatible with a long-time, experimental but resolute policy of changing the social order" (1926, p. 105). Self-direction, from a humanistic framework, is a clear example of the basic idea shared nearly seven decades ago by Lindeman.

Third, resistance to self-direction can sometimes be found in those educators who are strongly committed to a behaviorist foundation. One source of this criticism is that humanism does not easily lend itself to the measurement of observable performance. Humanism is concerned with the whole person, and this includes the affective domain (for example, attitudes and values) as well as performance. Reducing self-directed learning to a series of measurable objectives defeats the spirit of understanding the whole person and the unlimited potential that the person brings to the learning activity. Elsewhere, Hiemstra and I have made the case that because humanism and behaviorism share many common elements (such as emphasis on practical problem solving, the importance of previous experience, and the need to recognize that individuals enter a teaching-learning transaction with a wide range of knowledge and skills), there are ways to bridge the two paradigms in order to promote self-direction (Hiemstra and Brockett, 1994).

Conclusion

This chapter has been an attempt to clarify some of the myths and misunderstandings that can contribute to resistance among learners, instructors, and administrators toward principles and practices related to self-direction in adult learning. Unlike so many areas in the field of adult and continuing education, self-direction benefits from an extensive body of research and practice literature. While this literature is not without controversy and debate, it does fulfill an important function in that there is ample information to help limit the spread of myths that can give self-direction a bad name among educators of adults, regardless of the specific settings in which they practice.

References

Brockett, R. G. "Self-Directed Learning and the Hard-to-Reach Adult." *Lifelong Learning: The Adult Years,* 1983, 6 (8), 16–18.

Brockett, R. G., and Hiemstra, R. *Self-Direction in Adult Learning: Perspectives on Theory, Research, and Practice.* New York: Routledge & Kegan Paul, 1991.

Candy, P. C. *Self-Direction for Lifelong Learning: A Comprehensive Guide to Theory and Practice.* San Francisco: Jossey-Bass, 1991.

Elias, J. L., and Merriam, S. *Philosophical Foundations of Adult Education.* Malabar, Fla.: Krieger, 1980.

Hiemstra, R. "Self-Directed Learning: Individualizing Instruction." In H. B. Long and Associates, *Self-Directed Learning: Application and Theory.* Athens: Lifelong Learning Research/ Publication Project, Department of Adult Education, University of Georgia, 1988.

Hiemstra, R., and Brockett, R. G. "From Behaviorism to Humanism: Incorporating Self-Direction in Learning Concepts into the Instructional Design Process." In H. B. Long and Associates, *New Ideas About Self-Directed Learning.* Norman: Oklahoma Research Center for Continuing Professional and Higher Education, University of Oklahoma, 1994.

Houle, C. O. *The Inquiring Mind: A Study of the Adult Who Continues to Learn.* Madison: University of Wisconsin Press, 1961.

Johnstone, J.W.C., and Rivera, R. J. *Volunteers for Learning.* Hawthorne, N.Y.: Aldine, 1965.

Knowles, M. S. "Andragogy, Not Pedagogy!" *Adult Leadership,* 1968, *16,* 350–352.

Knowles, M. S. *The Modern Practice of Adult Education: Andragogy vs. Pedagogy.* New York: Association Press, 1970.

Lamont, C. *The Philosophy of Humanism.* (5th ed.) New York: Unger, 1965.

Lindeman, E. C. *The Meaning of Adult Education.* New York: Harvest House, 1926.

O'Hara, M. "Person-Centered Approach as Conscientização: The Works of Carl Rogers and Paulo Freire." *Journal of Humanistic Psychology,* 1989, *29* (1), 11–36.

Piskurich, G. M. *Self-Directed Learning: A Practical Guide to Design, Development, and Implementation.* San Francisco: Jossey-Bass, 1993.

Tough, A. M. *The Adult's Learning Projects.* (2nd ed.) Austin, Tex.: Learning Concepts, 1979.

RALPH G. BROCKETT is associate professor of adult education in the Leadership Studies Unit, University of Tennessee, Knoxville. He has been involved with self-direction in learning scholarship for fifteen years and is editor-in-chief of New Directions for Adult and Continuing Education.

Several key resources related to resistance and self-direction in learning are highlighted.

Resources Related to Overcoming Resistance to Self-Direction in Learning

Huey B. Long

Formal recognition of, and planning for, self-direction in learning (SDL) often constitutes a significant change in educational approaches. As a result, a high degree of intimidation is associated with its introduction to individuals who have no previous SDL experience. Thus, fear of the unknown, along with a reasonable satisfaction with the status quo, contributes to resistance. While the primary purpose of this chapter is to identify and report some resources that may contain helpful suggestions and ideas about overcoming resistance to SDL, several corollary objectives exist. In order to identify the literature, and to take appropriate action to overcome resistance, some parameters concerning the topic need to be established. Therefore, the following content is of three kinds. First, an effort is made to clarify critical terminology. Second, comments are made about theoretical aspects of resistance. Third, three dimensions of resistance are discussed briefly. A listing of selected resources is followed by a concluding comment.

Terminology

In the chapter title, the terms *overcome, resistance,* and *self-direction in learning* require clarification. The third term is defined first and then the other two are defined in order.

Self-direction in learning as defined by the editors is as follows: "Self-direction in learning refers to both the external characteristics of an instructional process and the internal characteristics of the learner where the individual assumes primary responsibility for a learning experience" (Brockett and Hiemstra, 1991, p. 24). While this writer does not believe that self-direction in learning is always associated with the external aspects of the instructional process, the definition above does not significantly affect the content of this chapter. My definition, as generally used, focuses on the learner's psychological processes that are purposively and consciously controlled, or directed, for the purpose of gaining knowledge and understanding, solving problems, and developing or strengthening a skill. Instructional activities may either facilitate or inhibit the process, but not necessarily cause or prevent it. In addition, SDL is frequently associated with goal setting, identification and selection of resources, and time management. Both definitions, however, address the implication that the learner engages in reflection, assessment, and evaluation as opposed to routinely and automatically accepting and internalizing information. Accordingly, SDL can occur in a classroom full of other learners as well as in a solitary model. Related terms include self-regulated learning and self-planned learning.

The words *overcome* and *resistance* each have their connotations. Overcome has three connotations: to conquer or defeat, to surmount or prevail over, and to overpower or exhaust. In the vernacular, overcome is endowed with a more active meaning than resistance. Resistance is defined as a force that opposes or retards. Even though resistance is frequently used in a negative way it also may have positive connotations. Consequently, as noted in Klein's (1969) chapter annotated below, resistance may be perceived as being "bad" or "good."

Thus, using the above definitions, overcoming resistance to SDL refers to removing or overpowering a force (resistance) that opposes or interferes with individuals' efforts to manifest responsibility and control over the learning process. Note that resistance is defined as an active construct rather a passive absence of something. This connotation of resistance is best understood in the framework of physics where resistance is conceptualized as a force such as friction that inhibits motion. Resistance to SDL may be analogous to the difficulty of launching a rocket into a space orbit. Thousands of pounds of thrust (energy) are required to overcome gravity. Metaphorically, the learner who resists self-direction in learning is anchored in an experience bounded by similar forces.

Some of the forces that retard the application and pursuit of self-directed learning are discussed in the following pages prior to the identification of resources. Three aspects of resistance are discussed below, as follows: locus of resistance, common sources of resistance, and strategies to overcome resistance.

Locus of Resistance

Resistance to SDL may be found in organizational structures and procedures, as well as among educators and trainers, and also among learners. As would be expected, the nature of resistance may vary among the three locations of resistance. Most of the literature concerning overcoming resistance focuses on the learner's resistance.

Organizations. Major organizations such as corporations, public schools, and higher education institutions have a long history of fostering dependent approaches to learning. These approaches are reflected by instructional techniques that emphasize recall, repetition, and memorization. Such organizations tend to prescribe roles for teachers, trainers, and professors so as to emphasize relationships and behaviors that intentionally limit learner initiatives. Whenever SDL is perceived to modify the traditional structure, personal roles, and status, resistance to it is common. An organization designed around passive learning practices will also be inclined to resist SDL as incompatible with its systems for grading and evaluating student progress.

Educators and Trainers. Educators and trainers are another source of resistance in the learner-teacher transaction. Their resistance emerges from several sources, including the tendency to prefer the familiar over the unfamiliar and the commitment to traditional platform instruction. Yet, the issue of control seems to be the major conceptual obstacle, or stated differently, the major source of resistance to the application of SDL. Lack of knowledge about SDL also leads educators and trainers to raise questions concerning their ability to apply SDL techniques.

Learners. Resistance to change is not limited to educators and trainers and organizations. Learners themselves are often as resistant to adopting SDL as their teachers. Hence, organizations, educators and trainers, and learners often constitute a powerful coalition to oppose SDL. Durr (1994) proposes that each of the above sources of resistance may operate from previously established paradigms that provide guidelines for behavior (Barker, 1988). It is implied that individuals will have to undergo a paradigm shift in order to become more accepting of SDL. Learners have multiple reasons for opposing SDL. After several years in school, learners (children and adults) adjust their paradigms to fit in with the system's paradigms. They also learn that didactic instruction that requires little or no thinking rewards passive, accepting memorization. Thus, reluctance to depart from past practice is coupled with fear of the unknown. More about resistance located within the learner is found in the resources identified in the following pages.

Common Sources of Resistance and Strategies to Overcome Them

Resistance to self-direction in learning is not limited to the location where it is found, as discussed above. It also seems to be rooted in some common human sources. Opposition to SDL may be described as emerging from emotions, understanding, and values.

Emotionally based resistance emerges from fear of the unknown, uncertainty about how to engage in SDL, and lack of confidence in one's ability to engage in a new kind of learning activity. An increasing body of literature is emerging that suggests willingness to engage in self-direction in learning is associated with self-efficacy. According to this hypothesis, the likelihood of engaging in self-direction in learning is positively associated with an individual's personal assessment of competence in given areas. Cognitive resistance is fueled by an existing paradigm of learning and an absence of knowledge about the meaning and processes of SDL. Currently, a variety of conceptualizations and definitions guide the offering of self-directed learning opportunities. Some of these may be meaningless and subsequently may be rejected. For example, self-directed learning is sometimes associated with pathological overemphasis on individualism, which limits its acceptability in group learning situations. Finally, at least as currently perceived by a number of individuals, pedagogical and other values may conflict with some concepts of SDL.

A variety of strategies may be employed to encourage SDL in existing organizations. These strategies may be informed by different social science change strategies. Kurt Lewin's (1951) Force Field theory appears to be basic to many strategies. In essence, this strategy employs techniques designed to reduce the negative forces while simultaneously strengthening positive forces. As noted above, most learners and agents are more comfortable with the status quo. According to Lewinian theory, the status quo is a the result of a balance between negative and positive forces. Hence, a change strategy must include awareness of some of the more powerful negative and positive forces that sustain the status quo of passive approaches to learning. Melioration strategies may be useful. See Grow (1991) for an example of this kind of strategy. Grow demonstrates an awareness that it may be difficult to move radically from a learning history based on passive approaches to more active SDL. Durr (1994) reports a strategy used in selected divisions of Motorola, Inc. to introduce self-directed learning procedures. Hiemstra and Sisco (1990) also counsel patience in the introduction and adoption of SDL.

Resources on Resistance to Self-Direction in Learning

The following constitutes only a small part of the literature available on overcoming resistance to self-direction in learning. The literature is extremely varied and voluminous. Works on the topic are found in Educational Resources Information Center (ERIC) reprints (identifiable in reference lists by "ED" followed by a six-digit number), adult education journals, business management journals, training literature, childhood education materials, and in a number of books published over the past twenty-five years.

The list could easily be doubled without diminishing the quality of the material. Therefore, three major criteria guided the selection: each item chosen contributed to the impression of breadth or variety of subjects and institutions, or demonstrated the range of publications or the diversity of discipline interest. Finally, when an item appeared in two places, the more comprehensive source was preferred. A major problem in the identification of resources was caused by the failure of two key concepts to be mutually exclusive. Procedures designed to enhance, develop, and strengthen SDL in some cases may also be ways of overcoming resistance to SDL. The former connotes a level of acceptance combined with lack of ability or knowledge of how to engage in self-directed learning. In contrast, the latter seems to address some kind of active resistance. Writers cited below do not always make such a distinction between the two conceptualizations.

Bandura, A. *Social Learning Theory.* Englewood Cliffs, N.J.: Prentice Hall, 1977.
  Bandura proposes a triadic reciprocal causation model of human behavior that provides some suggestions on how to overcome resistance to self-directed learning. According to the model, an individual is influenced by the interaction of his or her internal states, behavior, and environment. The construct of self-efficacy is a powerful force in the model. Furthermore, Bandura describes four major influences acting on self-efficacy: successful performance, vicarious experience, verbal persuasion such as praise, and emotional physiological arousal. See J. E. Jones (1994) for an application of Bandura's model.

Barell, J., Liebmann, R., and Sigel, I. "Fostering Thoughtful Self-Direction in Students." *Educational Leadership,* 1988, *45* (1), 14–17.
  Barell and his colleagues provide some grade-specific suggestions for elementary and secondary school teachers. They recommend that teachers create an environment where students have opportunities to observe each other thinking out loud, and to practice identifying problems, planning solutions, monitoring their own progress, and evaluating their own results. It is also important for students to learn critical thinking that respects others' viewpoints.

Brockett, R. G., and Hiemstra, R. *Self-Direction in Adult Learning: Perspectives on Theory, Research, and Practice.* New York: Routledge & Kegan Paul, 1991.
  Among other things, Brockett and Hiemstra discuss how self-directed learning can be facilitated. Strategies for enhancing learner self-direction are also noted. Other topics include research on the instruments developed by Guglielmino and by Oddi to assess aspects of self-directed learning attitudes. Additional chapters are devoted to topics such as policy and ethical issues.

Candy, P. C. *Self-Direction for Lifelong Learning: A Comprehensive Guide to Theory and Practice.* San Francisco: Jossey-Bass, 1991.
  Candy's 567-page book contains fifteen chapters that address various topics and issues in self-directed learning. Even though he does not specifically discuss ways of overcoming resistance to self-directed learning, he does identify variables that appear to be related to the enhancement of self-directed learning (p. 417). From the way the topic is presented, it appears that he may consider these variables appropriate in either of two circumstances: when the learner is not psychologically opposed to self-directed learning, and when resistance exists. The variables are competence, resources, and rights.

Confessore, G. J., and Long, H. B. *Abstracts of Literature in Self-Directed Learning 1983–1991.* Norman: Oklahoma Research Center for Continuing Professional and Higher Education, University of Oklahoma, 1992.

Confessore and Long provide 242 abstracts of articles, books, and chapters on self-directed learning published between 1983 and 1992. Many of the abstracts address ways of strengthening self-directed learning. The abstracts are indexed for easy identification by topic, subjects, instrumentation, and author. It is a useful reference tool.

Durr, R. "Integration of Self-Directed Learning into the Training and Education Process at Motorola." Paper presented at the 8th International Self-Directed Learning Symposium, West Palm Beach, Florida, Feb. 17–19, 1994.

Durr describes a procedure being used in the training department at the Motorola facility in Boynton Beach, Florida, to implement self-directed learning. He discusses how the training staff has attempted to reduce paradigm conflicts and facilitate the acceptance of self-direction in learning. Durr describes an individualized approach initiated by two departments within the organization. The process begins with a personally devised set of learning objectives. After the objectives have been identified by the employee, possible methods of accomplishing the objectives are explored. The employee-learner remains centrally involved in the process.

Godfrey, E. "Structuring Freedom: An Alternative Approach to Post-Graduate Course Design." *Management Education and Development,* 1983, *14* (1), 68–81.

Godfrey describes a three-term model used to progressively move students toward self-direction. She observes that students must be involved in changing content, ways of learning, and available resources. Godfrey also notes students must be able to negotiate individually what they do and how. In addition they must be involved in identifying evaluation procedures and criteria.

Grow, G. "The Staged Self-Directed Learning Model." In H. B. Long and Associates, *Self-Directed Learning: Consensus and Conflict.* Norman: Oklahoma Research Center for Continuing Professional and Higher Education, University of Oklahoma, 1991.

Grow developed what he calls the Staged Self-Direction Learning Model based on Paul Hershey and Kenneth Blanchard's theory of situational leadership. Grow's model also follows Lewinian theory concerning moderate change as opposed to radical change by indirectly changing the relationships between positive and negative forces in the life field. According to Grow, the teacher's role behavior changes as the learner progresses through four stages he calls dependent, interested, involved, and self-directed. In the first stage the teacher acts as authority source and coach, as a motivator and guide in the second stage, and as a facilitator in the third stage. Finally, the teacher serves as a consultant and delegator in the fourth stage. Examples and illustrations are included.

Hiemstra, R., and Sisco, B. *Individualizing Instruction: Making Learning Personal, Empowering, and Successful.* San Francisco: Jossey-Bass, 1990.

Hiemstra and Sisco's book is practical as opposed to theoretical. Based upon their combined thirty years of teaching experience, Hiemstra and Sisco describe how to individualize instruction. Only a few pages of the volume directly address how to overcome resistance to SDL, however. These pages contain specific comments concerning the problems presented by institutions, teachers, and learners.

Their suggestions are of two kinds: application and attitudinal. Application suggestions include self-revelation (by the teacher) about philosophy and awareness of the challenge SDL presents to some learners, and use of varied resources to engage learners' participation. Attitudinal suggestions include advice to teachers to trust in themselves and their students and to be patient.

Jones, J. E. "Self-Confidence and Self-Directed Learning: An Overview from Social-Cognitive Psychology." In H. B. Long and Associates, *New Ideas About Self-Directed Learning*. Norman: Oklahoma Research Center for Continuing Professional and Higher Education, University of Oklahoma, 1994.

Jones describes a process she uses in art classes for older adults. She identifies learner self-confidence and personal goals as major considerations in the development of self-directed learning. Based on her experience and on social-cognitive psychological theory, she proposes a set of guidelines for building self-efficacy that she indicates will result in increased learner acceptance of self-directed learning. Her guidelines include eight categories of teacher-learner collaboration that take place throughout the entire instructional process. Thirty-four specific acts are included in the eight activity categories.

Klein, D. "Some Notes on the Dynamics of Resistance to Change: The Defender Role." In W. G. Bennis, K. D. Benne, and R. Chin (eds.), *The Planning of Change*. New York: Holt, Rinehart & Winston, 1969.

Klein's chapter is particularly informative as he discusses resistance as a favorable behavior from the defender's point of view. The literature often represents resistance as "bad" because it is discussed from the change agent's perspective. According to Klein, resistance has an important benefit for the defender or object of change. It is used to protect the targets of change from threats to their integrity.

Kops, W. J. "Self-Planned Learning of Managers in an Organizational Context." In H. B. Long and Associates, *Emerging Perspectives of Self-Directed Learning*. Norman: Oklahoma Research Center for Continuing Professional and Higher Education, University of Oklahoma, 1993.

Kops reports a qualitative study of middle- and senior-level managers concerning self-planned learning of the middle-level managers in an organizational context. He discusses findings concerning self-planned learning efforts and organizational context before turning to an examination of the issue of modifying management training to accommodate self-planned learning. Of direct interest to this review is the identification of four conditions in the organization that diminish self-planned learning and six conditions that enhance self-planned learning.

Long, H. B., and Confessore, G. J. *Abstracts of Literature in Self-Directed Learning 1966–1982*. Norman: Oklahoma Research Center for Continuing Professional and Higher Education, University of Oklahoma, 1992.

Long and Confessore's 168-page book contains 141 abstracts of articles, books, and chapters on self-directed learning. Many of the abstracts include information on improving self-directed learning. The volume is indexed by several topics, including subjects, instruments, and type of publication. It is a useful reference tool.

Long, H. B., and Redding, T. R. *Self-Directed Learning Dissertation Abstracts 1966–1991*. Norman: Oklahoma Research Center for Continuing Professional and Higher Education, University of Oklahoma, 1991.

This 326-page book contains 173 master's and doctoral thesis abstracts concerning self-directed learning. Many of the abstracts refer to issues of enhancing and improving self-directed learning. Indexed for identification of abstracts by various topics, including subjects and instruments, the book is a useful reference document.

Lowry, C. M. "Supporting and Facilitating Self-Directed Learning," 1989. (ED 312 457)

Lowry identifies ten ways by which self-directed learning can be enhanced. Examples include encouraging learners to appreciate that they can act on their world individually or collectively to change it; negotiating learning contracts for goals, strategies, and evaluation criteria; providing examples of previously acceptable work; and helping learners to develop feelings of independence relative to learning.

Rodin, J. "Control by Any Other Name: Definitions, Concepts and Processes." In J. Rodin, C. Schooler, and K. W. Schaie (eds.), *Self-Directedness: Cause and Effect Throughout the Life Course*. Hillsdale, N.J.: Erlbaum, 1990.

Rodin and her colleagues emphasize the importance of control as a construct that affects a variety of personal actions. Following their premise, it can be argued that resistance to SDL may be in some way located within the learner's need for control. Learners who resist SDL because they are unfamiliar with it may be signaling acceptance of the passive teaching-learning situation because they have learned what they can control and what they can't. Therefore, they prefer the safety of being controlled in known areas to the uncertainty of greater control in unknown areas. Rodin and her colleagues identify three processes important to learning: cognitive processes, motivations, and emotions. Resistance to SDL can seem to the student to be a defense of self-direction itself, when the student's life course has shaped an expectation that learning is and ought to be an essentially passive activity.

Watson, G. "Resistance to Change." In W. G. Bennis, K. D. Benne, and R. Chin (eds.), *The Planning of Change.* New York: Holt, Rinehart & Winston, 1969.

Watson's chapter provides a general theoretical discussion of Lewinian theory of change. He bases his presentation on the assumption that an interaction between the force for change and the subject is required to successfully overcome resistance. He subscribes to the notion that resistance to change is best accomplished by neutralizing or transforming the negative forces to more positive ones and by strengthening the existing positive forces. Personal resistance to change is explained by complacency, preference for the familiar, dependence, self-distrust, insecurity, and other similar constructs. Social systems are influenced by similar variables. Hence, according to Watson's theory, the change agent must identify activities and ways to address these forces.

Conclusion

This chapter identifies some of the locations of resistance to self-direction in learning. Barriers to self-direction in learning may be found within organizations, educators and trainers, and learners. It is suggested that resistance may be explained in part by the conflict between existing paradigms and the self-direction-in-learning paradigm. Resistance in each of the three locations seems to emerge from common sources: emotions, understanding, and values. Only a few of the publications that address, directly or indirectly, the problem of overcoming resistance to self-direction in learning are described here. This chapter may be perceived as a sampler that represents the variety of views on the topic over a twenty-five-year time span.

References

Barker, J. A. *Discovering the Future: The Business of Paradigms.* St. Paul, Minn.: ILI Press, 1988.
Lewin, K. *Field Theory in Social Science.* New York: HarperCollins, 1951.

HUEY B. LONG is professor of adult education at the University of Oklahoma.

Portfolio assessment strategies hold great promise for promoting self-directed learning in formal classrooms. Art education provides examples for using portfolios; some implementation strategies are described.

Portfolio Assessment as a Strategy for Self-Direction in Learning

Jean Ellen Jones

Educational philosopher John Dewey (1916, 1986) made an important observation: Children and adults learn most naturally when they have a problem solving experience with relevant, real-life issues. Critical to that learning experience is skill in purposeful reflection. Several decades later, learning theorists under the constructivist banner have come to the same conclusions. By viewing learning as a construction of the individual, not something to be absorbed from teachers and texts, they are experimenting with a "portfolio assessment" approach to education. In this approach, problem-solving and student reflection, and their appropriate portrayal or documentation, receive primary attention.

Both learning theorists and practical adult educators are evoking strikingly parallel educational themes. Adult educators became interested in self-directedness through awareness of its central role in individual learning projects (Houle, 1961; Tough, 1971). This prevalent and natural approach to learning, while nearly universal, is far from well-developed in many adults. Much current discussion among adult educators centers around how self-directed learning can be developed in the formal classroom. Figuring prominently in the discussion are constructivist theory, problem-oriented learning, and reflective thinking (Candy, 1991; Boud, Keogh, and Walker, 1985).

For educational theorists who focus on traditional school-age students, self-directed learning is emerging as a serious interest reflected in educational research over the past twenty years. Pointing to the way people learn outside formal school settings as an appropriate model for in-school training, several such theorists have said that essential content should be determined and then authentic and meaningful problems should be devised using the content so that knowledge can be constructed. To make learning even more effective and to develop student feelings of control over their learning, teachers should also help students become "self-regulated" learners (Resnick, 1987, 1989).

Many of the tools used to realize self-regulated, intentional learning are coming from the arts. They are reflected in current language. Along with portfolio assessment, educators are urging the use of public performances, exhibitions, and examination of a student's repertoire. Even the instructional method of craft guild apprenticeship is being examined as a viable model (Collins, Brown, and Newman, 1989). The arts metaphor will be continued throughout this chapter with visual arts used as the model to describe recent practices.

Experiments with the portfolio format outside of visual arts have shown promise in isolated locations for some time. For example, the Bay Area Writing Project, begun in 1973, sparked widespread use of portfolio-like methods among writing teachers at every level, elementary through college, nationwide (Gray, 1986). A number of universities have used a portfolio for certification of skill levels from prior learning (Marsh and Lasky, 1984), as basic course work (Elbow and Belanoff, 1986), and as a component for student job interviews (Soares and Goldgehn, 1985). Such classroom-based uses of portfolios have even attracted the attention and support of the Educational Testing Service (Gitomer, Grosh, and Price, 1992).

Thus, portfolio methods have developed as important means for helping learners become self-regulated and gain some personal control. Those portfolio approaches currently being developed allow teachers and students to implement many of the strategies that have been associated with self-directed learning. Compare the following statement about self-directed learning with the description of the components of a portfolio below it.

> What differentiates self-directed learning from learning in more traditional formal settings is that *the learner chooses to assume the primary responsibility for planning, carrying out, and evaluating those learning experiences.* [Caffarella, 1993, p. 28; italics in original]

> A portfolio is a purposeful collection of student work that exhibits the student's efforts, progress, and achievements in one or more areas. The collection must include student participation in selecting contents, the criteria for selection, the criteria for judging merit, and evidence of student self-reflection. [Paulson, Paulson, and Meyer, 1991, p. 60]

This chapter explores portfolio assessment in formal educational settings. It also describes difficulties encountered with the portfolio process and ways they are being addressed. Among the solutions are several useful ideas for overcoming resistance to self-directed learning.

Portfolio Assessment in the Visual Arts

Art instructors are very concerned with building skills in self-directed learning so that, in the end, students can set their own goals and make their own "statements" (Eisner, 1972). Methods for helping students reach this end require learners to assume increasing amounts of control over the goals, processes, and evaluations of their work. Such art instruction calls for active commitment and problem-solving by students. Edwards (1989) and Huber (1989) provide useful models for typical high school and adult art teaching practices.

Although portfolio formats differ with every application and, indeed, every teacher, there are typical characteristics related to personal commitment, problem solving, and reflection that can be explored. The Arts PROPEL project provides a well-developed model (Winner and Simmons, 1992; Gitomer, Grosh, and Price, 1992). Funded by the Rockefeller Foundation in cooperation with the Educational Testing Service, Harvard Project Zero, and Pittsburgh Public Schools, PROPEL involved a five-year period (1987–1993) of experimentation with middle school and high school art teachers and their students. Many aspects of PROPEL are continuing through the support of local foundations and enthusiastic teachers.

The PROPEL approach uses many traditional methods of the visual arts discipline. PROPEL focuses on the production of art. Teacher and student agree on "domain projects" that require open-ended but guided, in-depth problem solving. Through involvement with concrete, visual problems, students become engaged in using the content of the discipline. Such content includes not only manipulation of materials, but training in analyzing their personal work, that of other artists, and the visual world.

Another component of the PROPEL approach, reflection, requires student artists to think about the learning processes they use and personal progress toward goals. This self-reflection occurs frequently during the problem-solving process and at the end of a project. It is also the main component for final assessment.

Art educators working in the PROPEL project found that the ways they implemented the general approach differed from teacher to teacher. Different teaching philosophies, students, course loads, and aspects of art being covered all influenced the formats used. There are several assessment approaches common to many PROPEL classrooms:

Setting public criteria

Keeping a portfolio of all work, including preliminary work and reflective writing, to be used as a reference point throughout the course

Individual and peer reflection, oral and written, often with guiding questions

Teacher feedback, oral and written, including teacher conferences

Checklists of project criteria with space for student and teacher evaluations and comments

Journals in which students frequently record their reflections, sometimes with guiding questions, at both a scheduled time and on their own time

Oral presentations to a significant other (such as a teacher, relative, or friend) of student-selected items and portfolio reflections, often including listener feedback via a questionnaire

Formal portfolio review, usually on selected projects. The portfolio typically includes an annotated table of contents, student background information, project work (including preliminary and trial work), journal entries, records of mid-term assessments by the teacher or student and teacher, and final reflective overviews of the work by the student, teacher, and perhaps, a significant other.
Portfolio-based exam.

In addition, as students engage in any reflective exercises, they and the teacher can judge the quality of their learning through examining statements about goals, documented progress toward goals, learning processes used, and personal or others' opinions.

Even though portfolio assessment methods are still being refined, they have generated enthusiasm among teachers who have tried them. For example, some teachers report that students are more motivated, express feelings of control over their learning, and are learning more about the subject and their learning processes. Other teachers add that they have increased their understanding of students and learned to clarify goals and expectations (Taylor, 1992; Winner and Rosenblatt, 1989).

Overcoming Problems with Portfolio Methods: Lessons for Self-Directed Learning

The continued need to refine portfolio methods is based on some problems that exist with the process. Led by teachers of writing, the most experienced with the process, educators from such disparate disciplines as visual art, math, science, instructional design, and adult vocational-technical programs are offering many similar suggestions for coping with difficulties and resistance. *Portfolio News* (1990–1993) is a primary vehicle for this ongoing discussion among teachers and administrators. Centra (1993) describes how teacher self-reports and portfolios can assist with various efforts to evaluate education.

By all accounts, portfolio assessment requires new strategies from teachers and students. When student confusion, apathy, or resistance occur, it is often because teachers have not adhered to basic assumptions about learning and teaching on which the portfolio process is based. For example, some attempt to use portfolio assessment methods while still teaching primarily through lectures and assigned textbook readings and exercises. Others fail to require self-reflection by students, who, without it, do not build sufficient ownership for their learning. Thus, teacher training pertaining to portfolios must be thorough and something more than a one-day, in-service meeting.

The early model developed by the Bay Area Writing Project continues to work well for helping teachers initiate the process (Gray, 1986). Using constructivist principles in teaching teachers, the Bay Area model stresses overcoming resistance through voluntary teacher experimentation with the process. Teachers, after hearing about basic principles and standard approaches, select a place to start in their own classrooms. As they try an approach, teachers reflect on the results and obtain feedback from fellow teachers and resource experts. This emphasizes teacher discoveries and helps build a better understanding of what really works. Trainers using this model have found that continuous contact among teachers is essential. A particularly useful element is regular meetings of teachers to assess student portfolios from all of their classrooms.

Even without a formal in-service program teachers can begin to obtain the direct experience that appears essential to overcoming resistance to portfolio assessment and self-directed learning. For instance, they can add the self-reflective components of portfolio assessment to any current learning project. Fingeret (1993), an adult literacy educator, reports that "The literature about preparing public school teachers to use portfolios is adamant on one central point: we learn by doing. So I began developing my own portfolio. It has been a powerful experience that leaves me a proponent of portfolio assessment on the basis of research, theory and my own experience" (p. 50).

Self-reflection, the core of the new process, requires careful attention. Teachers from various disciplines and settings report that students find it difficult to write self-reflective statements. Comments are often superficial and unconnected. Evaluators have noted that it is essential for students to see and discuss enough examples of good and bad performances, and useful and less useful learning methods, to build a basis for assessment comments. Very detailed written explanations assist students in making the transition to self-reflective processes. For example, one format builds portfolio instructions around questions often asked by students (Vermont Department of Education, 1991). Further, teachers must constantly model self-reflection statements and use student modeling as well where students examine each other's journals and portfolios. Students may practice by discussing their work in small groups before they write. Another solution has been to have students begin with a familiar process such as making judgmental statements, then justify and elaborate on their judgments.

Teachers and administrators alike have complained that the portfolio process is both more expensive and more time consuming than previous assessment methods. Besides the time spent learning the approach themselves, teachers note that they must give frequent feedback and collect and store a lot of paper. In the absence of administrative support for more released time from teaching duties, teachers have devised some time-efficient methods. Time spent presenting information to the group can be traded for more time with individuals. Trading group teaching duties with other teachers while conducting individual interviews also helps. Teachers can expand their effectiveness by using students, other teachers, and community persons to serve as resource and feedback agents. Other teachers may be especially helpful in training students to write self-reflectively.

Adult educators concerned with promoting self-directed learning in the formal classroom setting cannot afford to underestimate the rigor needed in implementing the portfolio approach. Unless the approach can be linked to high standards in a clear fashion, it will receive little respect or support from administrators or the general public. Several in the field of art education have dealt with past assessment problems and are currently working on reform (Alexander, 1993; Wiggins, 1993). Many people may not understand a discipline's dedication to a student-centered, problem-solving approach to education; however, they can understand a thorough assessment program and a well-illustrated report of learning outcomes.

Conclusion

This chapter has described how many of the behaviors and attitudes associated with adult self-directed learning are being used in the portfolio assessment process. By requiring students to take on personally relevant projects and then to reflect on their goals, progress, and processes of learning, teachers who use portfolio strategies are creating a dress rehearsal in the formal classroom for skills that will be useful for a lifetime.

Resistance to self-directed learning may be overcome in ways that have proven effective in addressing resistance to portfolio assessment processes. Training teachers thoroughly is essential. Such training should require teachers to include the reflective processes of portfolio assessment in their own learning. A second key component is training students to be self-reflective, including speaking and writing about personal assessments.

The wide-ranging experimentation with portfolio assessment by educators at all levels is very important in terms of contributions to the self-directed learning knowledge base. In addition, there are now many more educators developing resources for teaching self-directed learning and sharing strategies for overcoming resistance to it.

References

Alexander, F. "Standards: A New Opportunity for Arts Educators." In National Art Education Association, *Keynote Addresses: Art Across the Curriculum*. Reston, Va.: National Art Education Association, 1993.

Boud, D., Keogh, R., and Walker, D. (eds.). *Reflection: Turning Experience into Learning*. New York: Nichols, 1985.

Caffarella, R. S. "Self-Directed Learning." In S. B. Merriam (ed.), *An Update on Adult Learning Theory*. New Directions for Adult and Continuing Education, no. 57. San Francisco: Jossey-Bass, 1993.

Candy, P. C. *Self-Direction for Lifelong Learning: A Comprehensive Guide to Theory and Practice*. San Francisco: Jossey-Bass, 1991.

Centra, J. A. *Reflective Faculty Evaluation: Enhancing Teaching and Determining Faculty Effectiveness*. San Francisco: Jossey-Bass, 1993.

Collins, A., Brown, J. S., and Newman, S. E. "Cognitive Apprenticeship: Teaching the Crafts of Reading, Writing, and Mathematics." In L. B. Resnick (ed.), *Knowing, Learning, and Instruction*. Hillsdale, N.J.: Erlbaum, 1989.

Dewey, J. *Democracy and Education*. New York: Macmillan, 1916.

Dewey, J. "How We Think: A Restatement of the Relation of Reflective Thinking to the Educative Process." In J. Boydston (ed.), *John Dewey: The Later Works: 1925–1953*. Vol. 8: *1933*. Carbondale: Southern Illinois University Press, 1986.

Edwards, B. *Drawing on the Right Side of the Brain.* Los Angeles: Tarcher, 1989.

Eisner, E. *Educating Artistic Vision.* New York: Macmillan, 1972.

Elbow, P., and Belanoff, P. "Portfolios as a Substitute for Proficiency Examinations." *College Composition and Communication,* 1986, 37 (3), 336–339.

Fingeret, H. A. *It Belongs to Me.* Washington, D.C.: U.S. Department of Education, Division of Adult Education, 1993.

Gitomer, D., Grosh, D., and Price, K. "Portfolio Culture in Arts Education." *Art Education,* 1992, 45 (1), 7–15.

Gray, J. "University of California, Berkeley: The Bay Area Writing Project and the National Writing Project." In R. Fortune (ed.), *School-College Collaborative Programs in English.* Options for Teaching, no. 8. New York: Modern Language Association, 1986.

Houle, C. O. *The Inquiring Mind: A Study of the Adult Who Continues to Learn.* Madison: University of Wisconsin Press, 1961.

Huber, V. *Individuality and the Evening Art Course.* Unpublished manuscript, 1989. (Available from the author, 4009 Mandau Crescent, Madison, WI.)

Marsh, H. F., and Lasky, P. A. "The Professional Portfolio: Documentation of Prior Learning." *Nursing Outlook,* 1984, 32 (5), 264–267.

Paulson, F. L., Paulson, P. R., and Meyer, C. "What Makes a Portfolio a Portfolio?" *Educational Leadership,* 1991, 48 (5), 60–63.

Portfolio News. La Jolla: Teacher Education Program, University of California at San Diego, 1990–1993.

Resnick, L. B. "Learning in School and Out." *Educational Researcher,* 1987, 16 (9), 13–20.

Resnick, L. B. "Introduction." In L. B. Resnick (ed.), *Knowing, Learning, and Instruction.* Hillsdale, N.J.: Erlbaum, 1989.

Soares, E. J., and Goldgehn, L. A. "The Portfolio Approach to Business Communication." *Bulletin of the Association for Business Communications,* 1985, 48 (3), 17–21.

Taylor, P. "Visual Arts Portfolio: CAEA Pilot Project Update." *Portfolio News,* 1992, 4 (1), 7.

Tough, A. M. *The Adult's Learning Projects.* Toronto: Ontario Institute for Studies in Education, 1971.

Vermont Department of Education. *Your History as a Writer.* Montpelier: Vermont Department of Education, 1991.

Wiggins, G. "Assessment and Art Education." In National Art Education Association, *Keynote Addresses: Art Across the Curriculum.* Reston, Va.: National Art Education Association, 1993.

Winner, E., and Rosenblatt, E. "Tracking the Effects of the Portfolio Process: What Changes and When?" *Portfolio,* Dec. 13, 1989, pp. 21–26.

Winner, E., and Simmons, S. (eds.). *Arts PROPEL: A Handbook for Visual Arts.* Cambridge, Mass.: Harvard Project Zero, 1992.

JEAN ELLEN JONES is assistant professor of art education, School of Art and Design, Georgia State University, Atlanta.

*Various aspects of self-directed learning have been accepted as a
continuing professional education alternative for practitioners of
medicine in Canada and of architecture in the United States.*

Adopting Self-Directed Learning in Continuing Professional Education: Physicians and Architects

Gary J. Confessore, Sharon J. Confessore

In order to understand the nature and sources of resistance to self-directed
learning within professions, it is essential to differentiate between the participation of adults in education within general contexts and within professional
contexts. Hence, this chapter provides a cursory review of some concerns in
both contexts. It also describes two separate but related projects that have
introduced self-directed learning alternatives into mandatory continuing professional education systems: physicians and surgeons in Canada, and architects
in the United States.

An Overview of Participation in Adult Education

Houle's (1961) work is generally credited with having given rise to a flood of
scholarly works on participation in adult education. Over the years, some of
these studies have focused on characteristics of the individual, such as learning styles and motivation (Boshier, 1971; Burgess, 1971), while others have
focused on "attractors" and "deterrents" affecting participation (Aslanian and
Brickell, 1980; Cross, 1981; Scanlan and Darkenwald, 1984). In general, both
study types represent efforts to predict which individual adults are most likely
to participate in continuing education activities.

In a related genre, studies have been conducted to assess the role workplace challenges and opportunities play in individuals' learning activities.
These include Carnevale and Gainer (1989), Marsick and Watkins (1990),
and McGill, Slocum, and Lei (1992). Other studies directly concerned with

self-directed learning in the workplace include Confessore and Confessore (1993), Foucher (1993), and Guglielmino, Guglielmino, and Long (1987).

More central to the present chapter's concerns are works of those who have studied continuing learning activities of professionals. These include, among a great many others, Gross (1976), in pharmacy, and Hughes and others (1973) in medicine, law, theology, and social welfare. These works differentiate professionals from others in a variety of ways. Most are concerned with principles and techniques of presenting new information to professionals within the context of their status as adult learners. This includes accounting for individual learning styles, human and physical resources, and attractors and deterrents to participation. Two works in continuing medical education (Fox, Mazmanaian, and Putnam, 1989; Fox, 1991) and two by Schön (1983, 1987), who worked closely with architects, have been particularly influential in contributing to a reduction of resistance to self-directed learning in both fields. However, all four studies differ from those mentioned earlier in that they proceed from certain assumptions associated with professional status, although there does not appear to be one canonical definition of the term professional.

We believe much of the demand for formalized, even mandatory, systems of continuing professional education, and consequently some resistance to self-directed learning, is rooted in the evolving view of professionals held by society. Hence, the issue of professionalism will be considered in the next section.

What Is a Professional?

One important effort to provide an authoritative definition of the term professional, especially as it relates to educational concerns, was produced by Schein in 1970 as part of a series sponsored by The Carnegie Commission on Higher Education. He prefaced his list of ten criteria with the following caveat:

> Efforts at a clear definition of the concept of professionalism have had a long history. The problem of definition derives from our attempt to give precision to a social or occupational role that varies as a function of the setting within which it is performed, that is itself evolving, and that is perceived differently by different segments of society. Furthermore, the concept of the professional cannot be defined by any single criterion. Different sociologists have given different weights to different criteria, but all have agreed on the necessity to use a multiple criterion definition. . . . [p. 8]

Taken as a whole, Schein's criteria reflect what seems to have been an expectation of society that once an individual achieved professional status he or she retained it for the remainder of an active career. None of his criteria point to an expectation that professionals have a need to continue learning during the course of an active career. However, his assertion that professions are "evolving" and are "perceived differently by different segments of society" seems to reflect his concern that professional status in modern society was already under assault from external forces.

Schein's criteria for defining a profession are useful for purposes of this chapter because the expectation can be inferred, on the part of both professionals and society, that professional status is not to be questioned by those outside the profession throughout the period of an active career. No doubt many older citizens recall attributing something like Schein's criteria to clergy, physicians, and, perhaps, to lawyers until some forty years ago. Yet by 1970 there was already a well-documented inclination of society toward distrust of professionals. This inclination may have been stimulated by increased general awareness of personal and consumer rights, or by a greater sense of egalitarianism. However, it was most certainly magnified by a general awareness of the "knowledge explosion" and the realization that a professional's claim to possess specific, advanced knowledge could only be made in light of evidence that professional education was ongoing and effective (Curry, Wergin, and Associates, 1993).

In the midst of these complex forces, individual practicing professionals must attempt to balance their own motivations and insights with those of the public they are assumed to serve. Governments or regulatory bodies also are assumed, at least by the public, to be responsible for ensuring, in effect, that professional conduct comports with Schein's criteria and public trust.

The Professions Respond

It is somewhat ironic that by responding to such pressures and criteria through implementation of mandatory systems of professional education, professions have reasserted the positions that only professional peers should judge professional performance, that professionals possess a specialized body of knowledge and skills acquired during a period of lifelong learning, and that self-governing professional associations should define standards of education for continuing licensure. In the drive to mandate continuing professional education, the issues of objectivity, professional detachment, and mutual trust between the client and the professional seem to have remained unaddressed, along with the issue of the professional's potential self-interest.

As mandatory continuing education was implemented, the systems gravitated toward the bureaucratic convenience of counting credits rather than toward quality assurance. Continued licensure has been too often predicated on the number of hours spent in approved seminars or symposia rather than on evidence of actual learning. There has not been sufficient regard for where or how material was learned or whether it was likely to contribute to improved practice.

Mandatory continuing professional education systems have failed to establish in the public's mind that the primary motivation for professionals to continue learning is to improve their practice rather than to maintain their privileged status. This failure, more than anything else, seems to have been at the core of resistance to self-directed learning in the professions. Fortunately, as much as a decade ago, the literature began to include the very understanding that would cut this Gordian knot.

Schön's Concept of the Reflective Practitioner

Schön (1983) argues that we are in need of "inquiry into an epistemology of practice" that begins with the assumption "that competent practitioners usually know more than they can say. They exhibit a kind of knowing-in-practice, most of which is tacit. Nevertheless, starting with protocols of actual performance, it is possible to construct and test the models of knowing. Indeed, practitioners themselves often reveal a capacity for reflection on their intuitive knowing in the midst of action and sometimes use this capacity to cope with the unique, uncertain, and conflicting situations of practice" (pp. viii–ix).

In effect, Schön asserted that professionals develop the skills and habits of reflecting on any unfolding evidence of consequences (effects) stemming from actions taken (causes) as an integral dimension of the flow of practice, in order to function autonomously. Hence, his term "the reflective practitioner." By taking as his point of departure the synergistic interaction of practical competence and professional artistry, he laid a foundation for understanding that the unique and dynamic nature of any individual's practice is the best point from which to determine learning relevance.

In part, Schön's paradigm (1983) of reflection-in-action is a practical response to Schein's assertion (1970) that one of the hallmarks of any professional is an "ability to take a convergent knowledge base and convert it into professional services that are tailored to the *unique* requirements of the client system" (p. 45; italics in original). It is this notion that connects the nature of professionalism with reflection-in-action, and ultimately with the natural condition of self-directed learning among professionals. Although training for the professions inculcates a common knowledge or skill set, as soon as an individual engages in the professional activity of diagnosing and responding to specific needs of client cases that present themselves, the individual's practice becomes differentiated from that of others.

Schön (1983) attributes this effect to the fact that each case presents at least one of three features that prevents practice from becoming routine. These are uniqueness, conflict, and ambiguity. Hence, even within the context of a fairly narrow specialization, a professional obligation to tailor service to client requirements continually compounds the differences between one person's practice and another's. In the process of framing and reframing questions in an effort to understand the unique circumstances of each client, the reflective practitioner embarks on a road toward understanding or learning that becomes less and less amenable to support by generalized educational systems.

Self-Directed Learning as an Integral Function of Continuing Professional Education

In the area of continuing medical education, Fox (1991) agrees with much of Schön's concept of the reflective practitioner as descriptive of physicians. He reports, "Physicians I have talked to about this support the notion that in every case there is some aspect that is either unique, conflicted, or ambiguous" (p. 164). He also notes the motivation among physicians to change aspects of their practice is most often rooted in a passion to do a better job. This passion does not arise as a matter of feeling less competent than they should be. Rather, it reflects a desire to be as competent as they can be with regard to practice as they experience it (Fox, Mazmanaian, and Putnam, 1989).

Central among their findings, Fox, Mazmanaian, and Putnam (1989) report that it is changes in the lives and practice of physicians that precipitate the need to learn. This finding runs contrary to the traditional assumption that changes in practice follow episodes of learning. It also sheds a very different light on assumptions regarding motivational elements of traditional instructional designs.

Learning from practice is only a small part of the change physicians report. Most is accomplished by a process of self-directed learning in which "the overall plan is under the control of the physicians, even though many of the educational activities and resources used in the plan are developed by others. The pattern of formal and informal resources is what the learner controls, not necessarily the teaching or learning experience" (Fox, 1991, p. 156). In fact, change through learning among physicians involves reading, discussions with colleagues, and involvement in formal continuing professional education programs, in that order.

Similar distributions of learning activities are reported for several professions. Several researchers have focused on the issue of improved professional performance as differentiated from the accumulation of grades, credit earned, or hours of instruction endured (Benfield and others, 1977; Cervero and Rottet, 1984).

Overcoming the Resistance

Recently, two major continuing professional education projects have been undertaken with the expressed intention of incorporating Schön's (1983) reflective practitioner concept and the findings of Fox, Mazmanaian, and Putnam (1989). First was the Royal College of Physicians and Surgeons of Canada, who commissioned the Maintenance of Competency Project (MOCOMP). Within two years after that the American Institute of Architects commissioned the American Institute of Architects Continuing Education System (AIA/CES) project. Initial surveys of the membership of both professional associations yielded evidence that members were regularly engaging in self-directed learning activities in response to their need to improve practice. These learning activities were usually viewed as unrelated to formal continuing education. Many members were concerned that direct linking of documented traditional forms of continuing education with relicensure would not necessarily yield the desired evidences of improved practice. Moreover, in both surveys it was clear practitioners felt the existing system of continuing education did not address their unique and most pressing learning needs. Although almost none used the term, most called for a system that would grant full faith and credit for various forms of self-directed learning.

Addressing these concerns constituted a substantial departure from the status quo and required a comprehensive effort to identify and overcome resistance to change. Two critical elements of resistance were identified and efforts to overcome them were mobilized. The first was the momentum of past practice and the bureaucracy that had grown up around it. Each professional association had staff and policies empowered to support only traditional forms of continuing professional education. These activities represented a substantial source of income to the association. In order to overcome resistance to self-directed learning, it was necessary to disassociate issues of quality assurance from issues of centralized control. It also suggested the need for mechanisms to maintain an adequate stream of income. The second was the institutionalization of learning alternatives that responded to commonalities rather than differences in practice. Adapting to individual differences required educating the leadership and members regarding the validity of self-directed learning activities as measured in terms of improved practice. It also required development of systems by which self-directed learning can be recognized, recorded, and valued by the professional association.

A strategy of communication and education was undertaken by way of existing communications networks at the national, regional, and local levels. Using the results of surveys, both the leadership and the members were made aware of the extent to which they were already relying on self-directed learning activities as an important source of continuing professional education. In addition, information sessions and instructional materials were developed to assist the leadership and the members in their efforts to recognize and capitalize on opportunities to meet their unique learning needs. These materials included specific guidelines for organizing and conducting self-directed learning projects. As a result, a system was established that provided ways to meet unique individual needs while satisfying the association's need to validate learning among its members.

As yet untested is the argument that loss of income through provision of formal continuing professional education would be adequately offset by increased membership fees. This position is predicated on the assumption that membership in the professional association is valued in the context of the assurance that appropriate continuing professional education has been undertaken and accredited. To the extent that self-directed learning activities are seen as responsive to the unique needs of the practitioner, and are validated by the association, the value of membership will be enhanced in the eyes of individual practitioners. The result is an anticipated increase in membership income that will offset the loss associated with reductions in formally provided programs.

Conclusion

In order to overcome resistance to self-directed learning, leaders of the MOCOMP and AIA/CES projects undertook a strategy of long-term and profession-wide education designed to disseminate information regarding (1) the need for change in the continuing professional education system, (2) a full understanding of the historical antecedents of the existing system of continuing professional education, (3) the underlying construct of learning as it manifests itself among practicing professionals, and (4) the mechanisms by which incorporation of self-directed learning activities can satisfy the real need for change in practice rather than for renewal of license. However, the larger issue has been the establishment of an understanding that continuing professional education practices must link continued learning to improved practice. When that connection is made, the appropriateness of self-directed learning among professionals becomes self-evident and much resistance to self-direction is overcome.

References

Aslanian, C. B., and Brickell, H. M. *Americans in Transition: Life Changes as Reasons for Adult Learning.* New York: College Entrance Examination Board, 1980.

Benfield, W. R., Rosenbluth, S. A., Ryan, M. R., and Smith, M. C. "Detection of Early Warning Signs of Cancer by Community Pharmacists: An Evaluation of Training on Professional Behavior." *American Journal of Pharmaceutical Education,* 1977, *41,* 23–28.

Boshier, R. W. "Motivational Orientations of Adult Education Participants: A Factor-Analytic Exploration of Houle's Typology." *Adult Education,* 1971, *21,* 3–26.

Burgess, P. "Reasons for Adult Participation in Group Education Activities." *Adult Education,* 1971, *22,* 3–29.

Carnevale, A. P., and Gainer, L. J. *The Learning Experience.* Washington, D.C.: American Society for Training and Development and U.S. Department of Labor, 1989.

Cervero, R. M., and Rottet, S. "Analyzing the Effectiveness of Continuing Professional Education: An Exploratory Study." *Adult Education Quarterly,* 1984, *34,* 135–146.

Confessore, S. J., and Confessore, G. J. "The Extent and Nature of Employee-Initiated Learning in the Workplace." *Proceedings of the National Research Conference on Human Resource Development.* College Station: Department of Educational Human Resource Development, College of Education, Texas A&M University, 1993.

Cross, K. P. *Adults as Learners: Increasing Participation and Facilitating Learning.* San Francisco: Jossey-Bass, 1981.

Curry, L., Wergin, J. F., and Associates. *Educating Professionals: Responding to New Expectations for Competence and Accountability.* San Francisco: Jossey-Bass, 1993.

Foucher, R. "Factors Affecting Organizational Policies on Self-Directed Learning." Paper presented at the 7th International Symposium on Self-Directed Learning, West Palm Beach, Fla., Jan. 1993.

Fox, R. D. "New Research Agendas for CME: Organizing Principles for the Study of Self-Directed Curricula for Change." *Journal of Continuing Education in the Health Professions,* 1991, *11,* 155–167.

Fox, R. D., Mazmanaian, P. E., and Putnam, R. W. *Changing and Learning in the Lives of Physicians.* New York: Praeger, 1989.

Gross, S. M. "Demographic Study of the Relationship of Continuing Pharmaceutical Education to Selected Attitudinal- and Competence-Related Criteria." *American Journal of Pharmaceutical Education,* 1976, *40,* 141–148.

Guglielmino, P. J., Guglielmino, L. M., and Long, H. B. "Self-Directed Learning Readiness and Performance in the Workplace: Implications for Business, Industry, and Higher Education." *Higher Education,* 1987, *16,* 303–317.

Houle, C. O. *The Inquiring Mind: A Study of the Adult Who Continues to Learn.* Madison: University of Wisconsin Press, 1961. (Updated edition now available from the Research Center for Continuing Professional and Higher Education, University of Oklahoma, OCCE/200 McCarter Hall, Norman, OK 73037.)

Hughes, E. C., and others. *Education for the Professions of Medicine, Law, Theology, and Social Welfare.* New York: McGraw-Hill, 1973.

McGill, M., Slocum, J., and Lei, D. "Management Practices in Learning Organizations." *Management Dynamics,* Summer 1992, pp. 5–16.

Marsick, V. J., and Watkins, K. E. *Informal and Incidental Learning in the Workplace.* London: Routledge, 1990.

Scanlan, C. S., and Darkenwald, G. G. "Identifying Deterrents to Participation in Continuing Education." *Adult Education Quarterly,* 1984, *34,* 155–166.

Schein, E. H. *Professional Education: Some New Directions.* New York: McGraw-Hill, 1970.

Schön. D. A. *The Reflective Practitioner.* New York: Basic Books, 1983.

Schön, D. A. *Educating the Reflective Practitioner: Toward a New Design for Teaching and Learning in the Professions.* San Francisco: Jossey-Bass, 1987.

Gary J. Confessore is professor of higher education administration in the Graduate School of Education and Human Development at George Washington University, Washington, D.C.

Sharon J. Confessore is assistant professor of human resource development in the Graduate School of Education and Human Development at George Washington University, Washington, D.C.

Major factors supporting the increased use of self-direction in learning strategies in business and industry are presented, and the types of application are explored, with special emphasis on techniques for overcoming resistance to the new approaches.

Practical Experience with Self-Directed Learning in Business and Industry Human Resource Development

Lucy M. Guglielmino, Paul J. Guglielmino

There appear to be three major factors contributing to the increased interest in self-direction in learning in business and industry: unprecedented rates of technological and societal change that require increased flexibility and continuous learning, trends toward self-directed teams in the workplace, and research findings that consistently demonstrate a positive relationship between readiness for self-directed learning and performance.

Responding to these factors and other influences, human resource development (HRD) units in business and industry have begun to experiment with a variety of means of promoting self-direction in learning within their organizations (Motorola, Inc., n.d.). Richard Durr, manager of engineering and quality training for Motorola's Paging Products groups, provides a strong rationale for this position: "Self-directed approaches to training and development mesh with the philosophy of the learning organization. Gary Tooker, Motorola's president and chief operating officer, has pointed out that our continued success depends on our ability to hire and retain employees at every level who are 'motivated, bright, flexible, able to interact with their associates in participative and problem-solving teams and capable of continuous learning as our workplace changes.' Stand-up training is not the way to accomplish that goal" (phone conversation with the author, Oct. 1993).

In recent years, a wide spectrum of the business community has shown increased interest in self-direction in learning (SDL). Certainly not all companies are as advanced as Motorola; in fact, Motorola represents the leading edge in the adoption and adaptation of self-directed learning strategies. Winner of the prestigious and highly competitive Malcolm Baldrige award for exemplifying a company-wide commitment to quality, Motorola has recently dubbed itself "the learning company."

Some of the company literature reflects one reason for the business community's growing interest in self-direction in learning. With the increasing pace of change, it is no longer possible to train an employee to perform a finite number of job tasks. Motorola expects its employees to change and grow, assessing new developments (and needs for learning), determining how to gain the needed information and skills to make necessary adjustments, and moving on to the next challenge. While Motorola may be among the first companies to recognize the type of employee needed to deal with the rapid changes in this age of information and technology, it is far from unique in terms of the need to deal with the reality of constant, accelerating change.

In *The Futurist,* Cetron and Davis (1991) predict that today's technical knowledge will be only one percent of that available in the year 2050. This prediction alone implies a dramatic increase in training needs; but other experts predict that, in addition to rapid technological change, the trend toward changing jobs and careers will also continue. In *Workplace 2000,* Boyett (1991) foresees the average American entering the workforce in the 1990s working in ten or more different types of jobs and at least five different companies before retirement. Imagine some of the implications of this degree of change:

Those companies still relying largely on traditional "canned" training approaches may find themselves investing large amounts of funds in development costs only to realize that the materials are obsolete before or shortly after they are printed.

If more reliance is placed on stand-up trainers using a more interactive, fluid format, the obsolescence problem will be less severe, but cost is still a major issue. Training costs, in terms of both trainer salaries and trainee time, are rising at the same time more training is needed to deal with the rapid changes.

In some specializations, the rate of change is so rapid and the number to be trained so small that it is not feasible to use traditional approaches to training and development.

The rate of change during this era of rapidly expanding information and technology has been a major factor in the exploration of self-directed learning as a training and development option. Two other factors have also had a strong impact: the movement toward the use of self-directed teams to increase productivity, and research findings linking high levels of readiness for self-directed learning with higher job performance.

Current business literature chronicles the success of work teams as a means of motivating and energizing individuals and thus increasing productivity (Spencer, 1993). An in-depth examination of teams involving interviews with several hundred individuals working in fifty teams within thirty different companies and organizations led Katzenbach and Smith (1993) to observe that committed, effective teams naturally integrate performance and learning. These teams seek out what they need to know to get their jobs done, translating long-term goals into definable performance goals and then gathering the information and developing the skills necessary to meet those highly relevant goals. Comparing this description with Knowles's (1980) definition of the self-directed learning process, the similarities are striking. Just as Knowles contends that self-directed learning is more relevant and effective than traditional teaching, Katzenbach and Smith (1993) assert that teams functioning in this way not only produce superior team accomplishments and company-wide performance, but also spark individual development. Wellins, Byham, and Wilson (1991) state that self-directed work teams improve quality, customer service, and productivity, often dramatically, and that at least 26 percent of all organizations now make some use of self-directed work teams.

The third factor supporting the use of SDL strategies in business and industry is the discovery of a link between job performance and level of readiness for self-directed learning as measured by the Self-Directed Learning Readiness Scale (SDLRS). The SDLRS is a self-report inventory designed to assess a complex of characteristics supportive of self-directed learning (attitudes, perceptions, abilities). It has been translated into eight languages and used in more than twenty countries, with the majority of use, until recent years, in educational settings.

Most of the evidence of the link between SDLRS scores and job performance comes from three large studies conducted in major corporations. In 1980, Guglielmino and Guglielmino (1982) conducted a study in one of AT&T's operating companies, testing 753 individuals. In 1985, the study was replicated with a sample of 655 employees from the Hong Kong Telephone Company (Roberts, 1986). Most recently, Durr (1992) tested 606 Motorola employees. Each of these studies documented a significant positive relationship between performance ratings and SDLRS scores, a relationship that was significantly stronger for individuals whose jobs involved a high degree of change and required higher levels of creativity and problem solving. These studies support the logical assumption that workers who receive satisfactory and above-average performance ratings are those who are able to recognize needs for learning presented by a changing environment and devise means of obtaining the new information and skills needed to maintain performance and competitive position: they are self-directed learners.

Massive technological and societal changes, combined with the trend toward the use of self-directed teams, and research findings indicating a link between performance and readiness for self-directed learning have all contributed to the upsurge of interest in SDL in business and industry. How, then, have companies promoted the use of SDL strategies in the workplace?

The logical first step is to provide resources for self-directed learning at the job site. A study conducted in the highly technological aerospace industry (Rymell and Newsom, 1981) revealed that engineers were spending an average of 1,702 hours per year on learning projects, more than twice the number of hours devoted to learning projects by the average individual (816).

Not surprisingly, nearly half of the hours were spent on work-related projects; however, many of the employees reported difficulties and delays caused by inability to locate necessary information and other human and material resources for learning. Rymell concluded that employers benefit greatly from the self-directed learning of their employees, but do not always provide assistance, recognition, and resources to promote work-related self-directed learning. He points out that providing learning resources and support systems for self-directed learning would be likely to produce even greater gains for the company. Increasingly, companies are developing learning resource centers for their employees or expanding existing centers and staffing them with trained facilitators to assist in the location of needed information, materials, and services. A suggested list of resources for such a center was detailed several years ago (Guglielmino and Guglielmino, 1988), and an updated version is given here:

Data-search capabilities and assistance to retrieve specialized information from books and periodicals. Lockheed's on-line Dialog system, for example, allows the user to enter key words and immediately receive lists and abstracts of articles and books on the topic requested. Those used most frequently by the employees could be housed in the resource center; many already are in corporate libraries. In many companies, such as IBM, the entire data retrieval system is available at the employee's desk.

Audio-visual materials catalogued by topic. Many companies already own significant numbers of films and videotapes that are used in group training. In a learning resource center these would be available for individual use as well. Other companies are firm supporters of audiotaped instructional materials, especially for individuals in sales or others who travel a great deal. Cassette tapes can turn employee travel time into prime learning time.

Computer-assisted instructional materials and self-instructional texts. A wide variety of computer-assisted educational programs are now available, ranging from simple tutorials to interactive laser disk systems incorporating video and multiple-response capabilities such as touch screens. Their self-pacing and branching based on level of expertise, and their immediate feedback, make them valuable additions to a learning resource center. Many excellent self-instructional texts are also available, and many have been custom designed for specific areas of need, especially in health-care settings.

An index of individuals within the organization with expertise in specific areas. Access to one individual who is expert in a particular area can be worth more than dozens of books, articles, and videotapes. An index of this type becomes more important, of course, as the size of the organization increases and multiple sites are developed. The index can be tailored to the needs of the organization, expanding to include a regional or national listing if needed.

An index of available workshops, training sessions, and courses arranged by topic. These group training opportunities, once considered the heart of training and development, will remain an important training and development medium, but will become only one among many resources available for the self-directed learner. All locally available group training opportunities would be indexed, and most major corporations will include access to EDVENT, a computer data base offering current information on programs, courses, conferences, and workshops available throughout the United States and Canada. Many will also offer teleconferencing opportunities via satellite.

Consultation on learning plans and resources. The learning resource center would be staffed by facilitators who are familiar with the center's materials and data bases, as well as with self-directed learning processes. They would be available to discuss the individual's learning needs, assist in developing a learning plan (if necessary), and provide guidance in locating learning resources.

Facilities conducive to learning. Ideally, the learning resource center would provide a pleasant environment for learning. Individual study carrels, reading areas, areas for viewing videotapes or filmstrips or listening to cassettes, computers for utilizing computer-assisted instruction programs or other specialized software housed in the learning resource center, and small meeting rooms for group discussions are components that should be considered. Proper lighting is critical, and furnishings, color, plants, and layout should all be chosen with the creation of a comfortable learning environment in mind (see, for example, Hiemstra, 1991).

Four Strategies for Overcoming Resistance to Self-Direction in HRD Settings

Regardless of the quality of resources available, and the fact that much self-directed learning is already occurring in business and industry, attempts to promote widespread adoption of SDL strategies in business may be met with barriers ranging from apathy to outright resistance.

Awareness of Company Support for SDL. Sunoco management recognized that an essential element in the wider employment of SDL strategies in their organization was an awareness that this learning approach was strongly supported by the company. They therefore decided to provide orientation sessions for managers to familiarize them with the process, the company's commitment to it, and the resources available to managers and employees. (These resources included SDL facilitators who could assist in the location of needed information and materials.) Similar orientation sessions were incorporated into the initial training sessions for all new employees (J. Tuck, interview with the author, March 1986).

Internal Promotion. To maximize the use of SDL strategies, several companies have made strong efforts to provide reminders of the resources available: new videotapes or other self-study resources are highlighted in employee newsletters; presentations describing resources of particular interest are made at department or division meetings; the CEO or division chief mentions the money-saving innovation that began with a customized data search. Attractive posters or displays of learning resources are set up in high-traffic areas near entrances or time clocks, and in areas where traditional classroom training is conducted. Instructors of traditional training sessions can also point out resource center materials that can enhance or expand the knowledge gained or help correct problems that surfaced, such as difficulties with writing or oral communication.

Easy Access. Through links with electronic data bases, many employees now are able to access and download an almost unlimited range of information without leaving their own desks. Modems connect them to university libraries or directly to resources such as EDVENT.

Many other specialized data bases exist as well; for example, Bisline, a Florida pilot project for the U.S. Census Bureau, allows subscribers on-line access to business and economic data from the United States and several other countries. Custom searches can also be ordered. The cost of links with such systems is often minimal and sometimes free. Companies that invest in these communication links for their employees are vastly expanding their resources for self-directed learning.

Formalization of the Use of SDL Strategies. Some companies have formalized the use of SDL strategies by incorporating contracts for self-directed learning into annual performance appraisal and planning meetings. Among them are Sunoco (J. Tuck, interview with the author, March 1986) and Motorola (R. Durr, phone conversation with the author, Oct. 1993).

Motorola has long been recognized for its commitment to continued learning for employees, requiring that each employee participate in a minimum of forty hours of training per year, but the corporation has recently made an even stronger commitment to reinforcing the value of SDL to the learning organization. In a pilot project in Boynton Beach, Florida, Motorola is now validating self-directed learning projects as a means of fulfilling the education requirement. Richard Durr, manager of engineering and quality training for the paging products group, comments on the benefits, both realized and potential: "The training is done in their place, at their time, at their speed. We have a twenty-four-hour operation in manufacturing where that can be a real plus. Using a self-directed approach also opens doors to a lot more training opportunities that we don't have available in a classroom format and allows us to serve smaller numbers with needed training. Our pilot project has been quite successful, and we are planning a major expansion of the learning laboratory" (personal communication with the author, Oct. 1993).

Conclusion

Organizational and technological change has forced many companies around the world to reexamine the way things are learned by employees. The float time of knowledge has had to become less in order for companies in this global economy to remain competitive. In essence, we have entered into a period of just-in-time training.

Many leading organizations are discovering that self-directed learning offers a means of remaining competitive in an era of increasing change. This approach to learning is tailor-made for today's environment. Its advantages are significant:

The learner manages the learning process in terms of what is to be learned, when it is to be learned, and how it is to be learned.
The learning is timed to coincide with the need to learn.
The learner is more motivated, as a general rule.
The costs of learning are greatly reduced.
The learning is more relevant, efficient, and effective.

While changed methods always meet with some resistance, the forces supporting increased use of SDL strategies in business and industry appear strong and unlikely to be diverted. The combination of economy and productivity resulting from the use of SDL strategies is likely to lead to a major and lasting change in the way training and development takes place in the leading organizations—the "learning organizations"—of this century and the next.

References

Boyett, J. H. *Workplace 2000: The Revolution Reshaping American Business.* New York: Dutton, 1991.

Cetron, M., and Davis, O. "Fifty Trends Shaping the World." *The Futurist,* Sept./Oct. 1991, pp. 11–21.

Durr, R. E. "An Examination of Readiness for Self-Directed Learning and Selected Personnel Variables at a Large Midwestern Electronics Development Manufacturing Corporation." Unpublished doctoral dissertation, Department of Educational Leadership, Florida Atlantic University, 1992.

Guglielmino, L. M., and Guglielmino, P. J. "Self-Directed Learning in Business and Industry: An Information Age Imperative." In H. B. Long and Associates, *Self-Directed Learning: Application and Theory.* Athens: Lifelong Learning Research/Publication Project, Department of Adult Education, University of Georgia, 1988.

Guglielmino, P. J., and Guglielmino, L. M. *An Examination of the Relationship Between Self-Directed Learning Readiness and Job Performance in a Major Utility.* Unpublished research report, Guglielmino and Associates, 1982.

Hiemstra, R. (ed.). *Creating Environments for Effective Adult Learning.* New Directions for Adult and Continuing Education, no. 50. San Francisco: Jossey-Bass, 1991.

Katzenbach, J., and Smith, D. *The Wisdom of Teams: Creating the High-Performance Organization.* Boston: Harvard Business School Press, 1993.

Knowles, M. S. *The Modern Practice of Adult Education: From Pedagogy to Andragogy.* (Revised ed.) New York: Cambridge, 1980.

Motorola, Inc. *The Crisis in American Education.* Schaumberg, Ill.: Motorola, Inc., n.d.

Roberts, D. G. "A Study of the Use of the Self-Directed Learning Readiness Scale as Related to Selected Organization Variables." *Dissertation Abstracts International, 47,* 1218A. Doctoral dissertation, University of Missouri at Kansas City, 1986.

Rymell, R., and Newsom, R. "Self-Directed Learning and HRD." *Training and Development Journal,* 1981, 35, 50–52.

Spencer, K. L. "Review of *The Wisdom of Teams: Creating the High-Performance Organization.*" *Academy of Management Executive,* 1993, 7, 100–102.

Wellins, R. S., Byham, W. C., and Wilson, J. M. *Empowered Teams: Creating Self-Directed Work Groups that Improve Quality, Productivity, and Participation.* San Francisco: Jossey-Bass, 1991.

Lucy M. Guglielmino is professor of adult and community education and chair of the Department of Educational Leadership at Florida Atlantic University.

Paul J. Guglielmino is director of the Stuart James Research Center in Florida Atlantic University's College of Business and is assistant professor of management.

The technical training context offers a broad range of potential barriers to self-directed learning. A new way to incorporate self-directed learning concepts into the technical training process at a national laboratory is presented.

Applying Self-Directed Learning Principles in the Technical Training of a High-Risk Industry

Constance C. Blackwood

Often, mandated continuing education (MCE) is interpreted as the opposite of voluntary education. MCE is described by Cross (1981) as a state or professional requirement that members of certain professions must meet to retain their licenses to practice. Voluntary or self-directed learning experiences as described by Ash (1985) and others are those where adults are involved in the planning, conduct, and evaluation of their own learning. In industry today, especially in high-risk industries that require specific education and training, there is a type of learning that is neither exclusively mandatory nor voluntary in nature. In the nuclear, medical, and airline industries, for example, there is public demand for assurance of expertise. Therefore, regulations and requirements demand training in specific areas. Workers involved in these industries also recognize the need for such assurances and to a certain extent voluntarily pursue education; however, most of the learning experiences provided by the employer are still met with resistance and detachment from learners.

Purpose

The purpose of this chapter is to explore the apparent dilemma that adults prefer to learn in an independent, self-directed fashion but must often learn by a mandated set of requirements. The chapter will explore conflicts between self-directed learning and mandatory education as well as look at the potential for compatibility. If the assumption is that adult learners want to have some degree of control over their learning experience but industry guidelines demand specific criteria for that same experience, how are the two opposing forces reconciled? The issue is how much control is placed in self-directed methods. If the instructor provides objectives, resources, and an exam, and allows the learners to use their own style to fill in the blanks, that is transferring control to the learner. Some learners lack the skill and motivation to be successful so instructors become more prescriptive.

With the end of the cold war the nuclear research industry is struggling for declining and increasingly competitive government funding. However, research and development for safer reactors, protection of the environment, and management of waste are still major missions of the Department of Energy. In the process of prioritizing effort and money, the training function, though critical, is extremely vulnerable. Management must reform training to become more responsive, cost effective, and efficient. They must show a valid return on the training investment. There is value in looking at the role self-directed learning philosophy and practice can play in the mandatory technical training that is found in high-risk industry.

In the earliest studies that defined self-directed learning as the adult education community now understands it, methodologies primarily targeted voluntary learning episodes. In fact, the recognized seminal study in self-directed learning by Johnstone and Rivera (1965) was titled *Volunteers for Learning*. The population discussed in this chapter, however, is often involuntarily drafted into learning. From a mandated education perspective, it is helpful to look at self-directed learning from a less limiting definition than that of a voluntary learning experience. Some broader definitions include those of Schuttenberg and Tracy (1987), who divided self-directed learning into three conceptual categories: skills, processes, and philosophies. The category of skills includes the notion that self-directed learning is a method of instruction (Brockett and Hiemstra, 1985, 1991), and a set of skills to be mastered (Knowles, 1975). Self-directed learning as a form of instruction, such as Brookfield's (1986) model of the teaching-learning transaction, is categorized as a process. Philosophies are reflected in works describing self-direction as a variable in the definition of adulthood (Knowles, 1973), a personality construct (Oddi, 1984), and as an active change in consciousness and motivation (Brookfield, 1985; Mezirow, 1981). In the context of mandatory training for workers, it seems to make the most sense to discuss self-directed learning as an instructional method.

The Worker

The description of the nuclear worker under discussion in this chapter is primarily the same as the one used by Hellyer and Schulman (1991). The worker is usually in production, blue collar, traditionally educated, and middle class. Although given much responsibility, the worker perceives himself or herself to be powerless and controlled. In terms of learning experiences, if the worker chooses to learn something, the learning is most often individualized and not focused on collective or group learning. A self-directed learning experience on the job is likely to be chosen as a way to influence life circumstances. The worker population observed is in the nuclear industry. Coupling these worker characteristics with Guglielmino's observation (cited in Zemke, 1980) that a traditional education decreases the desire to learn and leads people to over-value authority and undervalue self-directed learning gives a clue about the receptivity of workers to required education and self-directedness.

This population has a unique set of barriers to successful learning experiences. Worker training needs are too often determined by "whatever is essential to formulate and fulfill a successful corporate strategy" (Rosow and Zager, 1988). In industry, a clear return on investment that includes improved performance measures demands efficiency in the education of employees. Especially in high-risk industry, required learning comes in the form of certain skill and knowledge requirements defined by statutory or regulatory provisions, licensure and certification standards, and safety and risk management requirements. All of these categories are very prescribed in a contextual nature. For example, Federal regulating agencies often require that information be delivered by a certified instructor; they prescribe who must attend, how long and how often they must attend, the content they must receive, and the type of evaluation used to determine their success. This formula leaves little to work with in the area of self-direction. Not all adult learning experiences must be self-directed. However, if adults learn most effectively when they retain a certain amount of control over their learning, it is to the benefit of the educator to incorporate self-directed learning techniques whenever possible.

The Industry

The nuclear industry has a strong Navy history. Beginning in the 1950s, Admiral Hyman Rickover, architect of the nuclear navy, stressed rigorous training and developed a behaviorist training regimen that carried over into both the commercial nuclear power industry and the public research and development nuclear industry. Delivery of training was in a command and control mode and the rigor matched the consequence of error on the job. By the mid 1980s, with distancing of the naval influence, and fueled by public accountability cries following the Three Mile Island incident, performance-based training became the standard in the nuclear industry. Models of training methodology became objective based and results oriented. Training programs began to infuse some adult learning principles into their products, taking into account the workers' experience and need for relevance. However, both management and workers continued to discount learning that was self-directed. Although more humanistic in approach, the prescriptive nature of technical education remained, and was generally more teacher centered than learner centered.

In an attempt to more clearly define mandatory training, the Department of Energy (DOE) issued an order in 1989. The Training Accreditation Order (DOE 5480.18A) was established by DOE to assist in achieving excellence in the development and implementation of performance-based nuclear facility training programs. The training manuals clearly defined how training for the DOE nuclear community should be conducted. One of the major components of the development of training was the incorporation of adult learning principles into the training programs. The order and the accompanying manuals are now regarded as the industry standard for training. The notion of improving the conduct of training was also supported by the demand for efficiency from management, based on the assumption that training based on adult learning principles is more effective than traditional training. Nuclear industry technical training began to move out of the classroom and into new formats like required reading, preshift briefings, computer-based training, interactive video, and self-paced methodologies. Self-directed learning still played essentially no role in the industry. Resistance occurred primarily at the managerial levels, due to fears that loss of control would lead to noncompliance to regulation.

Resistance to Self-Directed Learning

Designers and developers of performance-based training methods in the nuclear industry build a section into their course design package called "the motivator" (U.S. Department of Energy, 1991). This section is designed to impress upon the learner the importance and relevance of the material about to be studied. The motivator is often designed around a "consequence of error" scenario and, as implied earlier, is based on company goals, not on the workers' goals. Unfortunately, no major studies have concluded that consequence of error or poor job performance have been identified as a primary motivator of adult learners. However, in most of the literature discussing self-directed learning, the motivation of the learner is key to choosing a self-directed learning format. Tough (1979) suggested that learners are not singularly motivated; rather they are motivated to learn because they anticipate multiple benefits. For example, consider these excerpts from my interview with a highly successful reactor operator regarding his motivation for mandated training:

> As an operator, I strongly preferred to learn reactor systems and theory on my own. I wanted control, I wanted to set my own pace and use my own methods. I was very motivated and did very well at it for the following reasons: I had a contract with a checklist to finish, pass an exam and oral board before I could obtain qualification. Qualification meant more money, responsibility, and the opportunity to advance. I did well because I knew how to study, I had good research skills and memorization techniques. I was disciplined and kept a steady pace. I was mechanically/systems oriented, I knew how machinery basically worked. I wasn't afraid to ask questions and seek help when needed. Mandatory training wasn't by itself demotivating, it was expected as part of the job. Motivation for me was clear directions, a checklist, books, and the freedom to use the available materials as I wanted. As long as there were goals and objectives, I was motivated.

Although I have not found this to be typical, it is an excellent example of the self-directed learner operating quite successfully in a highly structured and singularly focused environment with multiple expectations and motivations. In mandatory training and required education, motivations and outcomes are typically singular and focused in nature.

Other types of resistance occur when there is no model to follow. Most adult educators recognize that self-directed learning does not take place in isolation (for example, Brockett and Hiemstra, 1991). However, the singular implications of self-directed learning projects are contraindicated by the shift or team nature of the work and training in a high-risk nuclear environment. Individual achievement is often the measure of a successful education experience, but training a team requires a different way of measuring success both for the team and for the individuals in it. Ways to adapt self-directed learning to training teams can be found, but are limited. Group consensus can be reached to define purpose, pace, and method of training, but like other high-risk training, the objectives, content, and evaluation remain prescribed by management or regulation, and not by the consensus of the group.

Incorporating Self-Directed Learning into Mandated Training

There are several ways in which self-directed learning principles and practices can be encouraged and facilitated in high risk industries. It has been my experience in years of working with adults that they initially flounder when confronted with self-directed learning possibilities. Many workers in my experience have suggested that they are not interested in defining their own education. For example, the traditional way to teach basic physics at most National Laboratories is the classic classroom method with an instructor imparting wisdom and a group of learners (who are required to be there) taking notes. Success is measured by a test with a score of 80 percent or better. A self-directed alternative can be pictured, where plant management would wait for each reactor operator to realize that a better understanding of basic physics might improve performance. At this point in the operator's career, a "teachable moment" (Havinghurst, 1952) has arrived, and as a result the operator begins to seek out information about physics. The first example creates an artificial rigidity that prevents optimal learning from taking place. The second example is not acceptable because the high risk and regulatory nature of the job cannot wait for each individual to arrive at the teachable moment. Both are extremes, but there lies some middle ground that can satisfy both needs.

I have had success when the academic infrastructure and expectations are prepared for the learners in a way that allows them to make choices from within a set of parameters. The microcomponents discussed by Hiemstra elsewhere in this volume offer one approach to facilitating this process. The following ten steps are offered as a strategy for successfully incorporating self-directed learning techniques into mandated education and training:

Educate management. Help managers interpret mandates liberally so that the need is met in the most cost-effective way. Ensure support by helping managers find out about the theory and advantages of self-directed learning.

Emphasize the optimization of learning and the efficiency of using self-directed learning principles.

Involve workers. Consider strategies that include the workers from the beginning by placing them on the curriculum committee, having them review regulations and requirements and help define the training plan for each individual job classification.

Know the audience. Survey the workforce with pointed questions like, What does it take to get this job done? How should a course be designed to help teach this skill or knowledge?

Incorporate audience feedback into the training plan. If the workers lack learning skills or are not ready to learn by self-direction, the first step is to help them acquire these skills.

Obtain learner support. Review the training plan with the workers and the supervisors. Answer any questions and negotiate changes. Job incumbents should be responsible for their own training and learning.

Be a consistent facilitator. Be honest and available. Once the parameters are set do not waver from them. Conti (1989) found that learners responded well academically to teachers who were consistent in their application irrespective of their teaching style.

Use contracts or plans. Use a learning contract at the very beginning of each class. Union workers especially understand and appreciate contract negotiations and they realize they are playing an important planning role. As demonstrated earlier, learners are motivated by learning plans that include checklists, procedures, end goals or objectives, and adequate materials.

Motivate workers. Because of the mandatory nature of some education, learners do not always see what the benefit is to them. Therefore, spend as much time as possible on motivating the learner. Make sure the learner is aware of benefits, which can include things like improved pay and chances for promotion or mobility, as well as increased self-esteem, resulting from mastery of the class material.

Incorporate alternative methods. Mandated learning experiences often take place in the classroom, which is extremely costly and has a low return on investment. Prepare alternative means of delivery such as reading, video, classroom, one-on-one mentoring, resource centers, study guides, modified on-the-job training, university classes, or test-out, and then give learners choices and options. To optimize self-directed learning, workers need to have materials available when they want them. Keep the training and resource centers open and staffed. Allow materials to leave the facility. Make the material so readily accessible that a learner might look something up simply because it is in easy reach.

Build the infrastructure. Know what is mandated, that is, what must be included in training by requirement or regulation, and set parameters. Arrange for a place that is a safe and appropriate environment. Build a basic outline of different topics. Gather resource materials and alternate teaching methods and materials. Train yourself; take train-the-trainer courses and learn as much as possible, not only about the topics but about what to expect from adult learners. Be sure to include plenty of independent practice options for learners to learn at their own pace.

Evaluate. If there is a mandated or standard test at the end, teach to the test. Interpret mandatory evaluation criteria as liberally as possible. Allow learners to choose how they would like to be evaluated whenever possible.

In a self-directed approach to individualizing instruction, Hiemstra and Sisco (1990) give a guide to practical application of several learning activity resources and approaches. These resources are the kinds of materials that should be included in any well-stocked adult learning center, along with written or human guides to their use, or both.

Conclusion

Even in the most highly structured learning environments, there are opportunities to practice self-directed learning. Overcoming barriers and dealing with resistance to self-directed learning can be accomplished by applying specific SDL techniques to the training program. Understanding the learner as well as your own teaching style are two profitable pieces of knowledge to begin the process. Wanting to learn and having to learn are compatible; the key lies in learner motivation and teacher understanding.

References

Ash, C. R. "Applying Principles of Self-Directed Learning in the Health Professions." In S. Brookfield (ed.), *Self-Directed Learning: From Theory to Practice.* New Directions for Continuing Education, no. 25. San Francisco: Jossey-Bass, 1985.

Brockett, R. G., and Hiemstra, R. "Bridging the Theory-Practice Gap in Self-Directed Learning." In S. Brookfield (ed.), *Self-Directed Learning: From Theory to Practice.* New Directions for Continuing Education, no. 25. San Francisco: Jossey-Bass, 1985.

Brockett, R. G., and Hiemstra, R. *Self-Direction in Adult Learning: Perspectives on Theory, Research, and Practice.* New York: Routledge & Kegan Paul, 1991.

Brookfield, S. D. "A Critical Definition of Adult Education." *Adult Education Quarterly,* 1985, 36, 44–49.

Brookfield, S. D. *Understanding and Facilitating Adult Learning: A Comprehensive Analysis of Principles and Effective Practices.* San Francisco: Jossey-Bass, 1986.

Conti, G. J. "Assessing Teaching Styles in Continuing Education." In E. Hayes (ed.), *Effective Teaching Styles.* New Directions for Continuing Education, no. 43. San Francisco: Jossey-Bass, 1989.

Cross, K. P. *Adults as Learners: Increasing Participation and Facilitating Learning.* San Francisco: Jossey-Bass, 1981.

Havinghurst, R. J. *Developmental Tasks and Education.* (3rd ed.) New York: McKay, 1952.

Hellyer, M. R., and Schulman, B. "Worker's Education." In S. B. Merriam and P. M. Cunningham (eds.), *Handbook of Adult and Continuing Education.* San Francisco: Jossey-Bass, 1989.

Hiemstra, R., and Sisco, B. *Individualizing Instruction: Making Learning Personal, Empowering, and Successful.* San Francisco: Jossey-Bass, 1990.

Johnstone, J.W.C., and Rivera, R. J. *Volunteers for Learning.* Hawthorne, N.Y.: Aldine, 1965.

Knowles, M. S. *The Adult Learner: A Neglected Species.* Houston, Tex.: Gulf, 1973.

Knowles, M. S. *Self-Directed Learning: A Guide for Learners and Teachers.* Chicago: AP/Follett, 1975.

Mezirow, J. "A Critical Theory of Adult Learning and Education." *Adult Education,* 1981, *32,* 142–151.

Oddi, L. F. "Development of an Instrument to Measure Self-Directed Continuing Learning." Unpublished doctoral dissertation, Department of Education, Northern Illinois University, 1984.

Rosow, J. M., and Zager, R. *Training—the Competitive Edge: Introducing New Technology into the Workplace.* San Francisco: Jossey-Bass, 1988.

Schuttenberg, E. M., and Tracy, S. J. "The Role of the Adult Educator in Fostering Self-Directed Learning." *Lifelong Learning: An Omnibus of Practice and Research,* 1987, *10* (5), 4–6, 9.

Tough, A. M. *The Adult's Learning Projects.* (2nd ed.) Austin, Tex.: Learning Concepts, 1979.

U.S. Department of Energy, Assistant Secretary for Nuclear Energy. *Training Accreditation Program Manuals.* DOE/NE–0102T, July 1991.

Zemke, R. "Learning to Learn: Survival Skill for the '80s Manager." *Training,* Nov. 1980, pp. 6–8.

CONSTANCE C. BLACKWOOD is director of academic programs at the Idaho National Engineering Laboratory. She has been involved in technical training at the Advanced Test Reactor and in DOE reactor training accreditation for over five years.

Career advisement via electronic mail, coupled with accessible data bases of job descriptions, local college programs, and regional learning providers, facilitates self-directed learning for career management at Niagara Mohawk Power Corporation.

Using Technology to Provide Self-Directed Learning Options for Power Utility Employees

Thomas D. Phelan

For years, human resource specialists in corporations have paid attention to the career paths of employees and implemented corresponding training and education programs. More recently, the focus has been on matching in-house and corporate-supported training and education to business plans. In addition, downsizing has left fewer human resource specialists to be concerned with employees' careers, and many employees are now responsible for managing their own careers (Sturman, 1990). With the new emphasis on employee-directed career management, the need for self-directed learners in corporate settings has become greater. In short, employees need to take charge of their futures, and corporations can help by providing the kinds of learner support systems that self-directed learners require.

Though human resource specialists may be able to predict a corporation's skill needs for the next few years, they typically do not know the true interests and desires of individual employees with regard to career development. Thus, most employees need career development techniques that help them determine their career paths and estimate the skills a corporation will need so they can direct their own training and education toward meeting future challenges. Self-directed learners therefore will have a distinct advantage in preparing for the careers of the near and distant future.

Personal Computer Facilitation of Self-Directed Career Management

At Niagara Mohawk Power Corporation in upstate New York, the personal computer (PC) has proven to be an effective tool for providing employee-paced methods of accessing career and educational information. At Niagara Mohawk, all employees are offered the opportunity to attend a general career development workshop consisting of two four-hour sessions one week apart, focusing on the fundamental principles of career development. The workshop is highly interactive, providing employees with an opportunity to develop networks with others. Spouses and significant others are invited to attend. Some employees bring older sons and daughters, especially those about to enter college or the job market.

PC-based tools are used in various ways to facilitate the workshop. For example, seven to ten days prior to the first session, participants are sent a pre-workshop package containing the input sheets for a PC-based assessment tool called "Successful Career Planning" (Bonnstetter, 1989). The data are collected and entered into a computer by career development staff between the first and second sessions. Software created by Bonnstetter (1989) produces an eight to twelve-page individualized profile based on the DISC instrument developed from Marston's work (1928). The instrument draws its name from the first letter of the first word in four defined areas that are examined: Drive-Challenge, Influencing-Contacts, Steadiness-Consistency, and Compliance-Constraints. The profile focuses on employee feelings about the present work environment and an ideal environment.

The benefit to corporations in using such an assessment lies in improved employee attitudes. Employees who understand their strengths and how those strengths contribute to success in their jobs are more apt to feel satisfaction in their present positions. "If your current employer offers what you want, you will probably be more committed to the organization and will work harder" (Fox, 1992, p.12). However, without the assistance of a PC, processing the reports in narrative form and in a timely fashion would be impossible. Niagara Mohawk's Career Development personnel have processed over a thousand profiles, delivering each to the individual employee at the second session of the workshop.

As employees enter the investigation stage of career development, personal computers also play a role as they look for specific information about the corporation and any requirements for future jobs. Once employees understand the requirements, they want information about strategies they can use to gain the appropriate skills, knowledge, and competencies through on-the-job training, job enrichment, or formal education. To facilitate the necessary planning process, Niagara Mohawk's Career Development unit has designed a career resource system using PC-based, user-friendly programs. The system helps career development specialists answer specific questions about training and educational opportunities.

For example, when employees need information about local college or university programs, they can use the internally developed "Guide to Colleges and Universities Within Our Service Territory." This guide lists key information about nearly sixty institutions of higher learning located in the company's upstate New York service territory, including a regional index, maps, and glossary of college terms. It is organized by the company's eight corporate regions with the goal of providing employees information about colleges within an hour's drive of home or work.

The entire guide is available through a PC. Employees can access information quickly through the system and then request printed copies. This includes such information as name and mailing address of the college, phone numbers, contact persons, type of institution, calendar, admissions, degree and certificate programs, special programs (adult or nontraditional programs), tuition information, and financial aid opportunities. Employees advance through each screen at their own pace. They can choose to limit their selection to colleges located close to home or to look at information about colleges in any or all of the eight regions. The information is updated annually.

In addition to general college catalogue information, PCs are utilized to provide a data base of schedules for college classes and also for high school and regional vocational-technical classes. Through a partnership with the Regional Learning Service, a Syracuse-based career counseling organization, Niagara Mohawk provides employees a computer-based schedule of such courses throughout the five-county region surrounding its corporate headquarters. They can locate classes by course title or subject. The information displayed includes school, location, schedule, costs, and contact person with a phone number. These data are updated every three months.

An additional feature of the program is called Distance Learn. Provided by the State University of New York's Regents College, Distance Learn is an index to college and university distance learning courses across the country. Again, employees search for courses by topic and are provided with information about media necessary to participate in the course, the school offering the course, a contact person's name and address, and the Regents College equivalent of the course for credit purposes. This is very useful for employees seeking to study at home or to complete degree requirements when prior study has been fragmented or stretched over a long period of time.

Another career information service offered in PC-based format is a data base of 750 managerial job descriptions. Employees select managerial jobs within the corporation from a published alphabetical index or a screen menu, and a complete job description including knowledge, competencies, and skills required for the position is printed.

At Niagara Mohawk there is also one mainframe application that has been recently established for assisting employees with career development advisement. Many employees have been E-mail users via the mainframe for department communication purposes. The advisement began when Career Development staff posted an E-mail message to all graduates of a general career development workshop, informing them of an opportunity to raise questions with career development specialists via E-mail. Response was immediate. Face-to-face career advisement sessions are still offered when requested or deemed necessary but the popularity of E-mail advisement has saved the Career Development Department considerable travel time and expense.

Although not currently used at Niagara Mohawk, there is another PC-based system that appears very promising for self-directed learners. This is the on-line course catalogue offered by Nova Southeastern University's Center for Computing and Information Sciences. Nova Southeastern offers college courses across the country via various nontraditional delivery techniques. Specialists there have made their entire eighty-page course catalogue available over the Internet. An interested person can send an E-mail request to cciscat@alpha.acast.nova.edu to receive the catalogue. The entire process is automated and receipt of the catalogue takes less than a half hour. As this innovation becomes replicated by other institutions, self-directed learners will be further assisted in their efforts to locate appropriate learning experiences.

Career Development and Self-Directed Learning

This career development program also provides employees at all levels of the organization with knowledge and skills basic to a career management process. The process has five steps: assessment, investigation, matching, choosing developmental targets, and "Managing Your Career With P-O-W-E-R" (Sturman, 1991). All five process components involve the presentation of choices to participants so they can see there is more than one way to develop a career.

Actually, there are many ways to manage or develop a career. For each employee, determining best how to contribute to a corporation's overall mission is the goal of career development efforts. The desired result is sometimes called "Job Fit." Employees want satisfaction and recognition from their jobs. At Niagara Mohawk, career development is defined as a systematized approach to having the right people in the right jobs at the right time, while providing opportunities for growth and development. This is a win-win situation for both the organization and the people involved, who both benefit when employees are satisfied and productive.

Assessment. In the assessment phase of the process, employees are exposed to twelve different self-assessment tools, such as the Successful Career Planning assessment tool discussed earlier, the Myers-Briggs Type Indicator (Myers, 1987), Career Codes (Holland, 1985), and Career Anchor (Schein, 1985). These measures provide a comprehensive assessment and a range of choices for each employee to consider. The idea is that, before investigating career opportunities, employees should first understand themselves, their needs, and their desires. It is also important to identify development needs not yet satisfied such as specific college degrees or technical skills.

Investigation. Following the assessment component, participants investigate the organization. Although some career development workshops teach employees how to investigate other industries as well as their home industry, the workshop at Niagara Mohawk is concerned only with investigating career opportunities within the corporation. Employees can certainly adapt the process to situations outside the organization, but the intention is to develop people for internal business needs.

After providing information on investigation methods such as networking and informal interviewing, specific job information is provided to employees. A listing of nearly 750 management job titles is presented to participants, who can request copies of job descriptions for those in which they are most interested. Here the PC plays a big role. In a single laptop, all 750 job descriptions and salary ranges are loaded and ready to print from a menu. Employees are provided with job descriptions either on the spot or within a week of the request. In addition, lists of union positions are included and employees can request copies of the most recent posting of any job and review the qualifications. Formal training requirements for all these positions are indexed and also available.

The organization chart, fifty-three pages in length, is also presented, offering with opportunities for identifying key managers in departments of an employee's choice. Employees are given an opportunity to study the organization's structure and help identify areas of growth and reduction. Lively workshop discussions and an idea-stimulation technique (Pike, 1990) encourage participants to investigate the possibility of future openings. The activity encourages self-directedness as each participant is required to address personal views of the corporation and its future and share ideas with others. It also emphasizes the need to assess the corporate situation before bidding for a new position.

Matching. The transition from investigation to matching is a very natural step. After assessing personal strengths and development needs and investigating the opportunities within the corporation, a natural question is, Where will my special contributions fit in? Matching is the process by which employees discover the best job fit and in a self-directed manner determine corresponding training and educational needs. In this component, employees are also asked to select a career strategy that will position them for a move toward greater career satisfaction, recognition, and contribution.

Choosing Developmental Targets. Choosing a developmental target is the next component. Here employees are discouraged from choosing a target that is too narrow, such as the job held by a specific individual. Instead they are encouraged to plan their development around job families and identify transferable skills applicable to a range of positions. This not only provides for career choice flexibility, but helps employees understand the corporation's bigger picture. In the long run, they are more valuable to the organization because of this broader preparation and understanding.

Managing Your Career with P-O-W-E-R. Once the target or area of greatest need is identified, employees are encouraged to manage their careers with "P-O-W-E-R" (Sturman, 1991). The "P" stands for planning development, "O" is for obtaining input from others, "W" is for working the plan, "E" is for evaluating results, and "R" is for revising as needed. Executing such a plan is complex due to a number of variables. Items that might change include such factors as the company's direction and the employee's educational plans, finances, family responsibilities, and skills valued. The important thing for employees to realize as they manage their own career development is that change will occur. A career plan must be monitored frequently and adjusted accordingly.

Importance of Self-Directed Learning

Self-directed learning in such a process has a distinct advantage. As noted earlier, corporations are becoming increasingly less able to do career planning for all employees. The matching of individual strengths, interests, and satisfactions normally must be done by an individual employee. Thus, charting educational and training plans becomes a highly individual matter.

In essence, career development is one area where corporations must encourage self-directed learning and be willing to support it. A career development workshop program is one positive step. A well-publicized in-house training program, accessible to all employees, is another. Tuition assistance programs can also increase self-directed learning because the in-house training program is extended by the resources of the educative community (Hiemstra, 1993) and self-directed employees can choose from a multitude of instructional providers. In the case of Niagara Mohawk, the Aid to Education program opens doors to the nearly sixty colleges and universities within the company's service territory, but does not restrict employees to them.

Career counseling is another way for the corporation to support self-directed learning. At Niagara Mohawk a number of self-directed learners set up career advisement sessions or contact career development specialists by E-mail with their questions. By seeking out this information, they are demonstrating their self-directed learning skills.

Overcoming Resistance to Self-Directed Learning

When employees are faced with career planning in difficult times, they need to acquire knowledge, skills, and competencies, sometimes under great pressure. The more choices they have, the better able they are to match educational opportunities to their individual learning styles. For adult learners this is critical to sustaining interest and enhancing retention. At Niagara Mohawk self-directed learning has been fostered by increased choice; technology also has played a major role in providing various choices in career development.

In essence, the PC environment helped employees become more self-directed and overcome some of the resistance they had to learning about career choices. There also was some resistance to self-directed learning in terms of management apprehensions about employees controlling their own career development. All that was required was convincing managers to allow the use of technology by those for whom it is the best choice.

The result has been gratifying. The on-line college and university index has received an increasing number of users, resulting in more employees returning to school. Career development questions via E-mail have been surprising both in number and in content with a greater depth and breadth in the content of messages than anticipated. The system has even been expanded recently to include computer-mediated discussion groups in the customer service area and on-line academic support groups for participants in an in-house electrical engineering master's degree program.

Conclusion

In summary, corporations are changing rapidly and, in many cases, downsizing. Corporate employees are in a scramble to gear up for future performance demands. The quest for knowledge is underway, and the path is highly individual. Self-directed learners will be the survivors. Only individual employees can make the choices appropriate to their individual learning styles and lifestyles. Corporations cannot do it for them.

They can pave the way by supporting self-directed learning in the ways presented above. Corporations have an opportunity to use computer technology to meet the needs of self-directed learners at a time when the motivation to learn, retrain, and survive in the corporate world is unprecedented. Corporate managers need only realize that self-directed learners may be their most valuable resource.

References

Bonnstetter, W. *Successful Career Planning.* Scottsdale, Ariz.: Target, 1989.

Fox, P. G. *Thriving in Tough Times.* Hawthorne, N.J.: Career Press, 1992.

Hiemstra, R. *The Educative Community: Linking the Community, Education, and Family.* Syracuse, N.Y.: Syracuse University Adult Education Publications, 1993.

Holland, J. L. *Making Vocational Choices: A Theory of Careers.* Englewood Cliffs, N.J.: Prentice Hall, 1985.

Marston, W. M. *The Emotions of Normal People.* London: Paul, Trench, Trubner, 1928.

Myers, I. B. *Introduction to Type: A Description of the Theory and Applications of the Myers-Briggs Type Indicator.* Palo Alto, Calif.: Consulting Psychologists Press, 1987.

Pike, R. *Creative Training Techniques Handbook.* Minneapolis, Minn.: Lakewood Books, 1990.

Schein, E. H. *Career Anchors: Discovering Your Real Values.* San Diego: University Associates, 1985.

Sturman, G. M. *If You Knew Who You Were . . . You Could Be Who You Are!* Greenwich, Conn.: Bierman House, 1990.

Sturman, G. M. *Managing Your Career With Power.* Greenwich, Conn.: Bierman House, 1991.

THOMAS D. PHELAN is a career development specialist at Niagara Mohawk Power Corporation, Syracuse, New York, and a doctoral student in instructional design, development, and evaluation at Syracuse University.

Reasons for resistance to using an instrument to gather students'
perceptions of self-directed learning are investigated, and suggestions
for overcoming this resistance are presented.

Resistance by Educators to Using a Self-Directed Learning Perception Scale

Jane Pilling-Cormick

Few instruments appear to assess students' perceptions of what they are experiencing and feeling during the self-directed learning process. Research includes attempts to determine who is self-directed and which characteristics self-directedness is related to, but little time is spent examining the process of becoming self-directed (Cranton, 1992). In response to this need, the author created the Self-Directed Learning Test (Pilling, 1991), subsequently named the Self-Directed Learning Perception Scale (SDLPS). The instrument was developed with undergraduate students to compile students' perceptions of the process. Questions require students to respond using a combination of Likert scale and open-ended responses.

Surprisingly, resistance was experienced when approaching some adult educators about using the instrument. Various reasons were cited. For example, one educator stated that the college was undergoing a change in the procedure for evaluating research studies. Consequently, no decision was made. When the educator was approached a second time, there were several reasons given for this evaluation committee not yet being formed. On the third attempt, the response was "the instrument does not apply to my class." Another institution was approached and one instructor enthusiastically agreed to administer the instrument. However, others in his department dismissed the instrument by stating "the instrument does not apply to my class." These types of responses encouraged the researcher to search for reasons why some instructors were eager to administer the instrument while others were not. The question became: Given a tool to measure students' perception of self-directed learning, why is there resistance to using the instrument and how can educators be encouraged to consider it?

Reasons for Resistance

Resistance to self-directed learning is not new. Many experienced teachers are not using what has been learned in two decades of research (Hiemstra, 1992). Two reasons for this resistance are particularly relevant for the SDLPS: misconceptions about the term self-directed learning and discrepancies between educators' beliefs and practices.

Misconceptions About the Term *Self-Directed Learning*. The term self-directed learning has various meanings for different people and has been identified as a possible source of confusion (Candy, 1990; Bonham, 1989; Long, 1992). Some think of it in terms of personality characteristics while others believe it to be an instructional method (Hiemstra, 1992). As outlined by Ralph Brockett in Chapter One and Brockett and Hiemstra (1991), there are various myths related to the self-directed learning process. It is no wonder that some instructors will dismiss the SDLPS by immediately giving the response that the instrument is irrelevant for their use. They, like many others, are not sure what self-directed learning really is.

Discrepancy Between Beliefs and Practices. Instructors may find, as Argyris and Schön (1974) suggest, a gap between "theories-in-use" and "espoused theories." The theories that govern instructors' actions are different from the ones they say they believe. Instructors are often unaware of any discrepancies. For example, an instructor may believe that assessing students' perceptions is important because this belief is generally accepted in the field of adult education. In reality, the instructor may not be asking for students' perceptions and is thus not applying this theory in actual teaching practice. Educators can agree with a concept in theory, but freeze when asked to implement it. If this is the case, an educator asked to use such an instrument may think the idea sounds good, but actually using the instrument as part of the "theory-in-use" is another matter.

Myths About the SDLPS. To enable instructors to see the instrument for what it really is, myths about the SDLPS need to be addressed.

Myth 1: SDLPS implies change. Self-directed learning is new for many instructors, as is assessing students' perceptions of the process. Some believe that using the SDLPS will indicate change is necessary. Most instructors are more comfortable doing things they know how to do well (Brookfield, 1990) and they only want to assess students' perceptions about something they know they can do well. Resistance is then a reaction to the possibility of change rather than specifically to the idea of using the SDLPS or self-directed learning.

Myth 2: SDLPS threatens the traditional teacher role. Some instructors incorrectly believe the use of the SDLPS will remove them from the driver's seat. In most institutions we see instructors controlling all parts of the teaching and learning process (Hiemstra and Sisco, 1990). They decide what, how, and when material is to be taught. The students are there to be filled with knowledge and teachers decide what type of evaluation is necessary. It becomes a way of life for teachers. Student teachers in faculties of education are often taught that this is what their teaching job will be! They are comfortable doing this and do not want to use an instrument that threatens this role.

Myth 3: SDLPS is a test of teacher performance. Some incorrectly assume that the SDLPS is a course evaluation and in turn, a test of teacher performance. Course evaluations can be threatening experiences and some educators do not like this type of evaluation. Consequently, they consider any attempt to use such an instrument to be a waste of time. The typical scenario of "course evaluation" involves requesting students to fill out forms during the last class that are not returned directly to the instructor. After inserting the completed forms into a sealed envelope, a student volunteer returns the completed forms to the department. This secretive nature can be threatening to instructors who spend hours preparing lessons, setting tests, and marking papers. They may worry that students do not like what they are doing. If instructors believe the SDLPS to be a course evaluation, the negative response is not surprising. Instructors need to realize that the SDLPS does not judge the quality of teaching, but provides feedback on the self-directed learning process from the students' point of view.

Myth 4: Self-directed learning cannot be measured with a questionnaire format. The SDLPS is a questionnaire and the overuse of structured questionnaires may lead instructors to resist using it. They may simply be "questionnaired out." Some may debate the usefulness of the form of results obtained from this type of assessment (Candy, 1991). Statistical techniques are used to compile results from questionnaires and many feel this is too mathematical. There is also a danger of attaching too much meaning to the numbers generated. These difficulties may cause instructors to shy away from using the SDLPS. Yet questionnaires can be useful tools for receiving valuable feedback, as long as educators interpret the results with caution.

Myth 5: Student feedback is not valid. Resistance exists among those who believe the myth that student feedback is invalid. There is a large amount of literature cited by Cranton (1989) supporting the validity of this form of feedback. Questionnaires are shown to be stable over time (Murray, 1980), internally consistent (Hoffman, 1978), and have high inter-rater reliability (Marsh, 1982). Despite this support, there still may be resistance, which needs to be overcome. Students are a valuable source of information. There are things to be cautious about when interpreting student feedback, but this does not mean that this source of information should be disregarded.

Myth 6: Trying to measure self-directed learning is a waste of time. The process of self-directed learning itself does take time and this concern is mentioned by a number of people, including Brookfield (1988) and Brockett and Hiemstra (1991). Some instructors using the SDLPS fear that the administration of the instrument will take away even more precious time. In reality, the SDLPS will actually save time by making it easier for the instructor to implement self-directed learning activities. Obtaining feedback from students can save instructors hours of time searching around in an attempt to figure out what students feel is and is not working. Having a tool can encourage those who do not use self-directed learning to consider it because there are ways to help with the implementation of the process.

Techniques for Overcoming Resistance to Using the SDLPS

Brookfield (1990) recommends several techniques for overcoming learner resistance that can be modified and expanded to address teacher apprehension toward assessment of the self-directed learning process:

Determine if resistance to assessment is justified. Instructors may have valid reasons for resisting the use of the SDLPS. As Brookfield states, resistance is a complex phenomenon and determining what combination of factors is causing resistance becomes necessary. Discovering or clarifying discrepancies between beliefs and practices is vital. We often think one thing and do another. Using critical thinking techniques to investigate instructors' assumptions and beliefs will help reveal any discrepancies. Encouraging instructors to become aware of possible gaps can help them determine if the resistance toward the SDLPS is justified.

Admit the normality of resistance. It should be no surprise that some educators feel initial resistance toward using the SDLPS; this resistance should be recognized as normal. It is common to feel resistance toward something strange and new. Educators should be encouraged to work through their resistance and the researcher should not feel offended or threatened because they do question the use of the instrument. Being understanding and providing opportunities to overcome this resistance will make the use of the SDLPS more effective.

Research teachers' background and cultures. Teachers come from various teaching backgrounds and cultures with a vast array of experiences. Their values, expectations, and cultural allegiances will have an effect on the way they view the use of the SDLPS. Those with previous unpleasant experiences using questionnaires may be reluctant to use them again. Someone who has taught in a traditional school may be reluctant to consider using the self-directed learning process, let alone administer an instrument that is even remotely related to it. Being aware of these influences can help shape the approach used when introducing the SDLPS.

Acknowledge the instructor's right to resist. Not all instructors prefer self-directed learning; it is fine to acknowledge that fact. As Brookfield (1986) states, every adult education program is a unique psychosocial drama. The cast of characters will never be exactly the same from one program to another. The selection of appropriate techniques depends on characteristics of the instructional situation, aspects of instruction being evaluated, and the sources of information being used (Cranton, 1989). As educators, we know each class is different and we do not use exactly the same techniques with all students. Students learn through various processes. Educators should be encouraged to determine the characteristics of their particular program that are conducive to self-directed learning. In doing so, they must be given the right to refuse to use the SDLPS and be respected for that decision.

Realize time is needed. Implementing a self-directed learning process cannot happen overnight. As Brookfield (1987) acknowledges, it took ten years of research and practice before he could admit to theory-practice contradictions he experienced when facilitating self-directed learning. Hiemstra and Sisco (1990) suggest that one should try using a process or technique at least three times before evaluating its effectiveness. The first time, the process will be new to both the educator and the learners. The second time, it will be new to only the learners. By the third time, it will be starting to be routine for the instructor, who can then assess the process and its impact. Instructors should be encouraged to adopt a similar outlook when considering self-directed learning and implementing the SDLPS. This will give them a chance to genuinely judge the instrument's usefulness.

Encourage educators to play an active role. Use of the SDLPS should be promoted, not as evaluation, but as a project in which educators are invited to play an active role. Many instructors and students progress well through the self-directed learning process. The SDLPS gives the opportunity for them to share perceptions of this successful interaction. Used in this way, the instrument is not threatening; it is a means of sharing and working together toward a common end: the facilitation of the self-directed learning process.

Explain intentions clearly and provide ongoing support. If the intentions of the SDLPS are not clearly stated, many instructors will continue to resist using it. What the instrument is, how it can be used, why it is used, and what it can do for the instructor all need to be presented in an easy-to-follow format. Hammond and Collins (1991) quote many sources to say that without careful orientation, learners may become defensive, threatened, or resistant to an idea. A similar argument can be made for educators. Aspects of the assessment may be ambiguous and the way the instrument is being used may be promoting resistance. Instructions for administration should be straightforward and instructors should be encouraged to question any aspect of the process.

Encourage sharing of success stories. Peer support for instructors and sharing personal stories of resistance toward assessment can be helpful. Former resisters are often very good advocates for the instrument. Someone who has felt the apprehension and has overcome it can identify with the fears of others who are resistant. If instructors can see that others are successfully using the SDLPS and are happy to be doing so, they will be more likely to overcome their resistance and try.

Some educators are successfully using other assessment techniques besides the SDLPS in their classes. Brockett and Hiemstra (1991) present one example of formative assessment to keep their teaching fresh and provide indications of how well the self-directed learning process is working for the students. This example confirms that process assessment can be used in some self-directed programs. We need to hear more about these stories. How do educators find them helpful? Why do they use instruments to assess their students?

Did they initially have fears about using such instruments? If they did, how did they overcome these fears?

Outline the practical implications of the SDLPS. It is argued that adult learners prefer practical information (Hiemstra and Sisco, 1990) and instructors are similar. Learners want something that they can put to use. Instructors also like things they can use immediately. If the introduction stresses practical ways the instrument can be used, instructors will be encouraged to use it.

• *SDLPS suggests possible reasons for students' problems with self-directed learning.* Process assessment enables the instructor to identify aspects that work or fail to work. Using the SDLPS will allow educators to modify their plans if feedback received indicates that their activities do not appear to be meeting the course goals. In this way, the results from the SDLPS help instructors customize their approach to the self-directed learning process to connect with where their students are coming from. Many difficulties can arise because of a "mismatch in perceptions or intentions of the parties involved" (Candy, 1991, p. 241). Perceptions change over the course of a program, and it is important for instructors to be aware of these changes. Instructors will be able to assess how self-directed learning is being perceived by their students and if an alternate way of presenting the self-directed process is required. In this way, they are in a better position to help them.

• *SDLPS can be used by committees.* The SDLPS can be an important tool for committees making decisions concerning courses. If the committee plans to offer courses that produce self-motivated, self-directed learners, some form of assessment is needed to determine if the committee is meeting its goals. The SDLPS offers a method of monitoring to see if these goals are being met.

• *SDLPS can help curriculum writers.* Curriculum writers or those responsible for program design could benefit from the SDLPS. If a program is to be self-directed, it must be perceived by the learner to be self-directed. Writers can use the SDLPS to obtain feedback when a program is implemented. Techniques often used by students when following a self-directed program are monitored. The SDLPS offers the possibility of determining the appropriateness of the course or characteristics of the course.

Conclusion

Educators need to see the rationale for asking about students' perceptions of the self-directed learning process. There is a continuing need for the development of alternative instruments to assess self-directed learning (Brockett and Hiemstra, 1991). The SDLPS is one of those instruments. Being aware of how students incorporate learning in the classroom with their individual learning is invaluable. There are no right and wrong answers. However, there is the opportunity for constructive feedback. Despite the need, there is resistance toward using this type of assessment that must be overcome. If resistance to using the SDLPS can be overcome, the apprehension toward using self-directed learning may also decrease.

References

Argyris, C., and Schön, D. A. *Theory in Practice: Increasing Professional Effectiveness.* San Francisco: Jossey-Bass, 1974.

Bonham, L. A. "Self-Directed Orientation Toward Learning: A Learning Style?" In H. B. Long and Associates, *Self-Directed Learning: Emerging Theory and Practice.* Norman: Oklahoma Research Center for Continuing Professional and Higher Education, University of Oklahoma, 1989.

Brockett, R. G., and Hiemstra, R. *Self-Direction in Adult Learning: Perspectives on Theory, Research, and Practice.* New York: Routledge & Kegan Paul, 1991.

Brookfield, S. D. *Understanding and Facilitating Adult Learning: A Comprehensive Analysis of Principles and Effective Practices.* San Francisco: Jossey-Bass, 1986.

Brookfield, S. D. *Developing Critical Thinkers: Challenging Adults to Explore Alternative Ways of Thinking and Acting.* San Francisco: Jossey-Bass, 1987.

Brookfield, S. D. "Conceptual, Methodological, and Practical Ambiguities in Self-Directed Learning." In H. B. Long and Associates, *Self-Directed Learning: Application and Theory.* Athens: Lifelong Learning Research/Publication Project, Department of Adult Education, University of Georgia, 1988.

Brookfield, S. D. *The Skillful Teacher: On Technique, Trust, and Responsiveness in the Classroom.* San Francisco: Jossey-Bass, 1990.

Candy, P. C. "The Transition from Learner-Control to Autodidaxy: More than Meets the Eye." In H. B. Long and Associates, *Advances in Research and Practice in Self-Directed Learning.* Norman: Oklahoma Research Center for Continuing Professional and Higher Education, University of Oklahoma, 1990.

Candy, P. C. *Self-Direction for Lifelong Learning: A Comprehensive Guide to Theory and Practice.* San Francisco: Jossey-Bass, 1991.

Cranton, P. *Planning Instruction for Adult Learners.* Toronto: Wall & Thompson, 1989.

Cranton, P. *Working with Adult Learners.* Toronto: Wall & Emerson, 1992.

Hammond, M., and Collins, R. *Self-Directed Learning: Critical Practice.* New York: Nichols/GP, 1991.

Hiemstra, R. "Individualizing the Instructional Process: What We Have Learned from Two Decades of Research on Self-Direction in Learning." In H. B. Long and Associates, *Self-Directed Learning: Application and Research.* Norman: Oklahoma Research Center for Continuing Professional and Higher Education, University of Oklahoma, 1992.

Hiemstra, R., and Sisco, B. *Individualizing Instruction: Making Learning Personal, Empowering, and Successful.* San Francisco: Jossey-Bass, 1990.

Hoffman, R. G. "Variables Affecting University Student Ratings of Instructor Behavior." *American Educational Research Journal,* 1978, *15,* 287–289.

Long, H. B. "Philosophical, Psychological and Practical Justifications for Studying Self-Direction in Learning." In H. B. Long and Associates, *Self-Directed Learning: Application and Research.* Norman: Oklahoma Research Center for Continuing Professional and Higher Education, University of Oklahoma, 1992.

Marsh, H. W. "Factors Affecting Students' Evaluations of the Same Course Taught by the Same Instructor on Different Occasions." *American Educational Research Journal,* 1982, *19,* 485–497.

Murray, H. *Evaluating University Teaching: A Review of Research.* Toronto: Ontario Confederation of University Faculty Associations, 1980.

Pilling, J. "The Assessment of Self-Directed Learning Among Pre-Service Students in an Ontario Faculty of Education." Unpublished master's thesis, Department of Graduate and Undergraduate Studies in Education, Brock University, 1991.

JANE PILLING-CORMICK *is a doctoral candidate in the Higher Education Group at the Ontario Institute for Studies in Education in Toronto, Canada.*

Adult educators may use a variety of techniques in formal learning situations to overcome learner—and teacher—resistance to self-direction in learning.

Enhancing Self-Direction in the Adult Learner: Instructional Techniques for Teachers and Trainers

Susan B. Slusarski

Does this sound familiar? I was facilitating some training in a major industry. The participants were meeting in small groups to list ways to reduce interruptions during work. The discussions were going well, so I was preparing materials for the next exercise. Juan, who had been quiet most of the session, left his group and approached me. Juan told me the session was going fine, but he really wasn't "into this working in groups. All you need to do, Sue, is tell me what to do, and I will do it." I thanked Juan for his input. He went back to his group. And my perspective on teaching adult learners had been irrevocably jarred.

Depending on one's perspective, it is possible to have interpreted this as a cultural issue: Juan was used to an instructional setting with the instructor as content expert and students doing what they were told. Or, one may view Juan as not ready to be a self-directed learner, unwilling to take responsibility for his own learning. Or, possibly, Juan really was telling me how he learned best! This critical incident made me reflect on my own teaching and view of self-direction in learning.

Self-directed learning has been discussed in three main ways in the past twenty years. Self-direction has been described as "a self-initiated process of learning that stresses the ability of individuals to plan and manage their own learning, an attribute or characteristic of learners with personal autonomy as its hallmark, and a way of organizing instruction in formal settings that allows for greater learner control" (Caffarella, 1993, pp. 25–26). This chapter discusses self-direction as a way of organizing instruction by examining the teacher, learner, and instructional process and by suggesting techniques that help overcome resistance to self-direction and permit greater learner control.

New Directions for Adult and Continuing Education, no. 64, Winter 1994 © Jossey-Bass Inc., Publishers

From Teacher to Facilitator

The teacher's traditional role is that of content expert. In this role, the teacher knows what should be learned and how to learn it; the teacher has responsibility for the learning. In self-directed learning, however, "the focus of learning is on the individual and self-development, with learners expected to assume primary responsibility for their own learning" (Caffarella, 1993, p. 26). If the student has the primary responsibility for learning, then what is the teacher's role?

In self-directed learning, the instructor's role changes from content expert to facilitator or guide (Brockett and Hiemstra, 1991; Candy, 1991; Knowles, 1980). Hiemstra and Sisco (1990) describe the change in the instructor's role from "content giver to learning manager, facilitator, and resource locator" (p. 5). This new role requires different skills of teachers and a different pattern of behavior in relation to their students. To make this transition, instructors should understand adults as learners, accept a humanistic philosophy, and let go of the traditional view of teacher control. Despite the new outlook, they need to be prepared to build learner control slowly.

Adults as Learners. The characteristics of adult learners have been described by Knowles in his andragogical model of teaching. These characteristics include the need to be self-directing, the possession of a wealth of previous experience and an intrinsic motivation for learning, and the preference for a task-centered orientation to learning (Knowles, 1980; Merriam and Caffarella, 1991). An understanding of these characteristics is basic to accepting a facilitative role with the adult learner.

Humanistic Philosophy. It is important, too, that instructors explore their philosophy of teaching, as self-direction in learning is based on a humanistic philosophical orientation (Hiemstra and Sisco, 1990). Facilitators provide learners with more than content, they are mentors giving vision, challenges, and support to learners (Daloz, 1986; McAlpine, 1992). Finally, the instructor takes a risk by being "an authentic human being with feelings, hopes, aspirations, insecurities, worries, strengths, and weaknesses" (Knowles, 1975, p. 33).

Sharing Control. To translate these beliefs into practice, instructors may begin by sharing control of the instructional process with learners. For example, arranging the classroom with small tables in a U-shape and starting with introductions brings learners together and sets a climate for shared control (Hiemstra, 1991). The facilitator may give choices—such as self-introduction, partner introduction, or introductions in small groups—on how introductions are conducted. Another technique would be for the group to interview the instructor. After breaking into smaller groups (where they would naturally start with their own introductions), each group develops questions and takes a turn interviewing the instructor. Questions are often about the course, but they may be personal as well. In this way, the instructor demonstrates openness and humanness. These approaches say to the learner, I am willing to share control of the learning with you. In Chapter Ten, Hiemstra describes several microcomponents of the teaching and learning process where learners can assume or share more control.

Facilitators may give learners some choices in instructional materials to be used. An instructor could provide several readings on a topic and students choose one that interests them. For example, in one workshop, I provided participants several copies of three different journal articles about professional development. After selecting one and reading it, participants grouped themselves by the article chosen and discussed the information. Then each group summarized their discussion for the larger group. This technique could be used in other ways, too. Rather than reading an article, learners could choose reading a book, interviewing three experts, or watching a video on the topic—different materials to accomplish the same learning objectives.

Some learners may initially resist taking some control and choose to have the teacher provide direction on what to learn and ways to go about learning (Pratt, 1989). As Schuttenberg and Tracy (1987) found, "some adults prefer direction in their learning process for reasons of efficiency, reliance on instructor expertise, or familiarity with traditional instructor-student roles" (p. 4). These may have been Juan's reasons for speaking to me during the training class. As Schuttenberg and Tracy suggest, "the overall strategy is to begin where the learners are" (1987, p. 6). The instructor may need to take more control at first. Then, as learners expand their repertoire of learning strategies and develop confidence in their learning abilities, facilitators may relinquish control.

The rewards for moving from teacher to facilitator of self-direction in learning are great. The instructor's role becomes "multidimensional, including being a facilitator, manager, resource guide, expert, friend, advocate, authority, coach, and mentor" (Hiemstra and Sisco, 1990, p. 61). In essence, the teacher becomes a co-learner with the learner.

Helping Learners Overcome Resistance

Perhaps one of the biggest reasons for resistance by adults to taking control or assuming self-directed learning is the conditioning of prior schooling. Many K–12 or college experiences were teacher-directed. Moreover, some of these experiences may have included highly competitive situations, belittling by an arrogant teacher, speed reading requirements, and cramming for tests.

Self-directed learning situations are different. They require learners to relate to peers collaboratively—to see peers as resources, giving and receiving help from them (Knowles, 1975). This may initially be confusing to some adults. As Taylor (1986) describes in a study on self-direction in a higher education classroom, "adults who subscribed to the *idea* of self-direction in learning but whose *experience* has been primarily teacher-directed formal education were faced with a discrepancy. . . . They found themselves in an intense struggle to grapple with disorientation and to develop an understanding and a way to deal with this 'new world of learning'" (p. 69; italics in original). How can facilitators help learners make the transition? Caffarella (1993) noted four variables that determine readiness for self-direction in learning: level of technical skills, familiarity with the subject matter, sense of personal competence as learners, and the context of the learning event. By examining these four variables as possible reasons for resistance, techniques can be used to decrease resistance and enhance learner self-direction.

Level of Technical Skills. Adult learners may resist self-direction in learning because they feel they lack technical skills not only in the subject matter but also to learn on their own. Readiness for self-direction includes having skills in goal setting, planning, self-management, and self-evaluation (Knowles, 1990). The missing skills can be identified by an inventory such as the SDLRS (Self-Directed Learning Readiness Scale) (Guglielmino, 1977) or the SDLPS (discussed by Pilling-Cormick in the preceding chapter), and then addressed by the facilitator through readings, class exercises, and ongoing feedback. For example, to build the technical skills of writing a book review, the facilitator may discuss how to review a book, distribute an article on writing book reviews, provide a model of a well-written book review, and then have the learners read and critique short book reviews before they write their own. In this way, learners develop the technical skills needed to perform the task.

Familiarity with the Subject Matter. When learning a subject area unfamiliar to them, students may resist taking control of their learning until they are more familiar with the subject. In a heuristic case study of adult views of their own learning, Ellsworth (1992) found that self-directedness varies with the subject matter being learned. With more intimidating subjects such as math or physics, adult students desired more teacher-directed situations. With familiar subject matter such as social relations or business, they desired more self-directed learning situations.

Facilitators may help learners feel more comfortable with a new topic by providing a frame of reference for course material. Michel (1992) suggests using a structured overview, graphics, or a conceptual map. The structured overview is an outline of the topics to be covered. Graphics representing the main concepts may be used as reference points or to introduce the material. Similarly, a conceptual map shows the relationships between concepts and provides a "schematic summary" (Michel, 1992, p. 18) of what is being learned.

Another technique is to encourage the learner to be less hesitant about the unfamiliar and to take risks. At conferences, I have encouraged participants at my session to attend subsequent conference sessions on topics unfamiliar to them. By learning to deal with the unfamiliar, adult learners develop confidence in their ability to handle new information.

Sense of Personal Competence as Learners. Adult learners need to view themselves as able to learn on their own. Ellsworth (1992) found that "confidence was cited as an almost necessary factor in engaging in self-directed learning" (p. 28). One technique for building confidence is to expose the learners to the concept of learning styles. By discussing different learning styles with learners or having them complete a learning style inventory, mismatches between their learning approach and instructional approaches used can be discussed. Often, when learners know their best learning style, they will have more control over the learning experience.

Another technique to help build learner confidence is to share the concept of "Smart Martian" with the learners. In their own environment, Martians are smart. Learners in a new learning experience are like Martians who arrive on Earth—quite capable but needing to learn how things are done on Earth. A Smart Martian attitude by facilitator and learner recognizes that the learner is competent and helps set a climate for a positive learning experience.

Context of the Learning Event. Many learners will need support to make the paradigm shift to a learner-centered context with a climate of mutual respect and trust. Having names on tent cards and using small group activities that encourage collaborative learning help build a supportive climate.

A different approach would be to change the learning context itself. Field trips help learners relate classroom work to the real world and recognize their capabilities in both situations. For example, members of an ESL (English for speakers of other languages) who have mastered check-writing in the classroom may go to a bank and write a check there. A comparable technique would be for learners to give a presentation in class and then give the same presentation in another class or to their co-workers or supervisor. By starting safe and then moving to a new context, learners may develop confidence in different contexts.

By building learning skills and learner confidence, providing a frame of reference for the material, and creating a supportive climate, the facilitator will help learners develop more responsibility for their learning.

The Instructional Process and the Learning Contract

The learning contract is frequently cited as a means to help learners gain control of the learning event by systematically planning subsequent activities, and to move from dependency to self-direction (Brockett and Hiemstra, 1991; Hiemstra and Sisco, 1990; Knowles, 1975, 1990; O'Donnell and Caffarella, 1990). Such contracts organize learning more effectively, provide a match between learner needs and training content, allow more creativity in identifying resources and developing strategies, and permit different kinds of evidence pertaining to accomplishments (Dejoy and Dejoy, 1987). Learners indicate what they will learn, how they will learn it, and how the learning will be evaluated. Introducing learning contracts gradually is one way to bolster learners' confidence in managing their own progress and accomplishments.

Deciding the What. Course objectives are integral to any learning. One technique to help learners take control of what they want to learn is to provide a diagnostic exercise or a model of desired competencies, so the learner has a guide to follow (Knowles, 1975). Another technique is to set the objectives in a context familiar and practical for the learner. In a GED class, for example, the objective may be to write a paragraph using a topic sentence and supporting points. However, the learning will be more effective when learners are given an opportunity to relate the objective to their own lives. Thus, learners in the process of job hunting could use the exercise to express in a written paragraph why they should be hired for a job, while learners who are expectant parents might use the same exercise to write out in paragraph form what needs to be done when a baby comes home from the hospital.

Similarly, if the goal is to develop language skills, the facilitator may have the learners generate the topics and themes. In an adult basic education class on developing language skills and examining cultural diversity, a facilitator provided copies of "My Name," a short essay about a girl's perspective of her Spanish name, Esperanza (Cisneros, 1988). Students read the essay and then wrote about the meaning of their own names. After sharing their writing, class members developed a list of themes to use for the next language experience. In this way, the facilitator provides learning opportunities based on the learners' experience that are both practical and pragmatic (Caffarella, 1993), and helps learners select specific content to match their learning needs.

Deciding the How. An instructor often provides resources for learners, directing them to a magazine or journal article or bringing in a pertinent book. However, greater learner control over this area would involve helping them identify and secure resources on their own. For example, learners could generate a list of resources for a given topic, including books, journals, audio tapes, videotapes, or programmed instruction materials (Dejoy and Dejoy, 1987). Someone may suggest subject matter experts or other learners (peers) or work supervisors who could be resources.

Accessing such resources may be new for learners. A brief discussion of where to obtain materials or how to request information from people may be necessary. Role-playing information interviews or taking a field trip to the library may provide learners with the confidence to try these methods on their own.

Typical ways of demonstrating learning are writing papers and reports. Learners may be given some choice in the format of a paper—perhaps writing a play or creating a case study—or in the time frame for completion. Other ways of showing evidence of learning include giving a presentation, making a poster, or filming a video. However, facilitators may need to provide how-to information for any of these techniques.

A special technique I like that provides evidence of learning and brings facilitator and learner into a collaborative relationship is journal writing. Through the journal, learners describe feelings, ask questions, react to classroom events, or share their personal lives with the facilitator. The facilitator may then offer encouragement, clarify misconceptions, or simply come to understand the learner's needs better. Thus, "the learner has increased private access to the instructor and considerable control over the agenda for the conversation" (McAlpine, 1992, p. 24).

Deciding How Well. Examinations are often required in learning situations. To give learners some control, the class could write some test questions. These questions then serve as a study guide for the test, and the examination is actually made from these questions. Or, the class could decide the most important areas in the content, and the facilitator develops the test from these areas.

Other verification of learning may come from feedback from the facilitator, the learner's supervisor, or the learners themselves. A facilitator often becomes the evaluator and in many cases is most familiar with the student and the learning objectives. In some circumstances, the learner's supervisor or a co-worker may be a more appropriate choice to verify the learning. In other circumstances, learners may do self-evaluations or assess their own performance on daily learning activities (Jurmo, 1989).

Learning contracts can provide a useful baseline for evaluation. However, learners may initially resist using such contracts, and it may be necessary to schedule a separate orientation session for learners. Here, the learning contract is examined as a learning process. The facilitator can "help trainees better understand the planning process, the idea of a learning contract, and the notion of their own learning style" and "foster their awareness of learning to learn concepts as a set of skills" (Dejoy and Dejoy, 1987, p. 66).

For learners who are more skilled, the decisions for all parts of the learning contract may be made by the learners with the facilitator providing support. Learners could read articles on how to use learning contracts or meet with a partner who has already worked with them. A panel could discuss their experiences with learning contracts—how they first felt about the approach, what some of the difficulties were, how they adjusted, and what they saw as the benefits. The facilitator might provide samples of learning contracts. Or, learners might meet in small groups and develop a contract for an imaginary student, sharing their products with the large group for feedback. Another technique would be to establish peer support groups during the course.

At first, the facilitator may need to provide many opportunities—topics, materials and resources, and activities—from which learners can choose to help build confidence and the skills to learn independently. Later, learners will have developed the skills to select their own topics, materials, and activities, alone or in collaboration with others.

Conclusion

For many teachers and trainers, encouraging learners to take control of their own learning has become paramount. Self-direction in learning "has become for many adult educators one of the major goals of their instructional processes: allowing and, in some cases, teaching adults how to take more responsibility and control in the learning process" (Caffarella, 1993, p. 29).

To accomplish this goal, instructors must view their role as that of facilitator—not content-giver, but guide and mentor. Learners will need to develop learning skills and confidence in their abilities as learners. Facilitators help by providing opportunities for learner decision making and learner control through the instructional techniques used.

Developing self-direction in learners is a worthy goal for any instructor. Self-direction provides a match between learner information needs and the learning content, develops motivation, improves learning skills, and helps learners respond to changing workplace requirements (Dejoy and Dejoy, 1987). Indeed, as Caffarella (1993) states, "the ability to be self-directed in one's learning, that is, to be primarily responsible and in control of what, where, and how one learns, is critical to survival and prosperity in a world of continuous personal, community, and societal changes" (p. 32).

References

Brockett, R. G., and Hiemstra, R. *Self-Direction in Adult Learning: Perspectives on Theory, Research, and Practice*. New York: Routledge & Kegan Paul, 1991.

Caffarella, R. S. "Self-Directed Learning." In S. B. Merriam (ed.), *An Update on Adult Learning Theory*. New Directions for Adult and Continuing Education, no. 57. San Francisco: Jossey-Bass, 1993.

Candy, P. C. *Self-Direction for Lifelong Learning: A Comprehensive Guide to Theory and Practice*. San Francisco: Jossey-Bass, 1991.

Cisneros, S. *The House on Mango Street*. Houston: Arto Publico Press, 1988.

Daloz, L. A. *Effective Teaching and Mentoring: Realizing the Transformational Power of Adult Learning Experiences*. San Francisco: Jossey-Bass, 1986.

Dejoy, J. K., and Dejoy, D. M. "Self-Directed Learning: The Time is Now." *Training and Development Journal*, 1987, 41 (9), 64–66.

Ellsworth, J. H. "Adults' Learning: The Voices of Experience." *MPAEA Journal of Adult Education*, 1992, 21 (1), 24–34.

Guglielmino, L. M. "Development of the Self-Directed Learning Readiness Scale." *Dissertation Abstracts International, 38*, 6467A. Doctoral dissertation, University of Georgia, 1977.

Hiemstra, R. (ed.). *Creating Environments for Effective Adult Learning*. New Directions for Adult and Continuing Education, no. 50. San Francisco: Jossey-Bass, 1991.

Hiemstra, R., and Sisco, B. *Individualizing Instruction: Making Learning Personal, Empowering, and Successful*. San Francisco: Jossey-Bass, 1990.

Jurmo, P. "Instruction and Management: Where Participatory Theory Is Put into Practice." In A. Fingeret and P. Jurmo (eds.), *Participatory Literacy Education*. New Directions for Continuing Education, no. 42. San Francisco: Jossey-Bass, 1989.

Knowles, M. S. *Self-Directed Learning*. New York: Association Press, 1975.

Knowles, M. S. *The Modern Practice of Adult Education: From Pedagogy to Andragogy*. (Revised ed.) New York: Cambridge, 1980.

Knowles, M. S. "Fostering Competence in Self-Directed Learning." In R. M. Smith and Associates, *Learning to Learn Across the Life Span*. San Francisco: Jossey-Bass, 1990.

McAlpine, L. "Learning to Reflect: Using Journals as Professional Conversations." *Adult Learning*, 1992, 3 (4), 15, 23–24.

Merriam, S. B., and Caffarella, R. S. *Learning in Adulthood: A Comprehensive Guide*. San Francisco: Jossey-Bass, 1991.

Michel, S. L. "Training 101:.Three Tools to Help Learners Learn." *Training and Development Journal*, 1992, 46 (6), 17–19.

O'Donnell, J. M., and Caffarella, R. S. "Learning Contracts." In M. W. Galbraith (ed.), *Adult Learning Methods: A Guide for Effective Instruction*. Malabar, Fla.: Krieger, 1990.

Pratt, D. D. "Three Stages of Teacher Competence: A Developmental Perspective." In E. Hayes (ed.), *Effective Teaching Styles*. New Directions for Continuing Education, no. 43. San Francisco: Jossey-Bass, 1989.

Schuttenberg, E. M., and Tracy, S. J. "The Role of the Adult Educator in Fostering Self-Directed Learning." *Lifelong Learning: An Omnibus of Practice and Research,* 1987, *10* (5), 4–6, 9.

Taylor, M. "Learning for Self-Direction in the Classroom: The Pattern of a Transition Process." *Studies in Higher Education,* 1986, *11* (1), 55–72.

SUSAN B. SLUSARSKI is an educational consultant and doctoral candidate in adult education at Syracuse University. Her research interests include the adult learner and the learning process, instructional strategies and techniques, and professional development.

Dividing the teaching and learning process into a series of micro-components makes it possible to ease the transition to self-directed learning by providing many small and nonthreatening opportunities for learners to make their own decisions.

Helping Learners Take Responsibility for Self-Directed Activities

Roger Hiemstra

Self-direction in learning has been practiced by many adult learners throughout history. One important finding emanating from self-directed learning research during the past twenty-five years has been that most learners prefer to take considerable responsibility for their own learning when given the opportunity. As Tough (1979) found, two-thirds of all adult learning activities are planned by learners themselves. He notes, "as an individual moves from the age of 10 to adulthood, the proportion of self-planned projects increases, and . . . reliance on a group decreases" (p. 85).

Assuming Personal Control over Learning Efforts

This knowledge that most adult learners desire to assume considerable responsibility has resulted in notions about empowering learners to take personal ownership for their own learning: "Adult learners are capable of taking personal responsibility for their own learning and assuming an increasingly larger role in the instructional process" (Hiemstra, 1992, p. 327). The assumption of more control over the teaching and learning process has had a profound impact on the way some people think about instruction. For example, Knowles (1984) identified several strategies for enhancing an individual's control over the whole learning process. I and my colleague, Burt Sisco (1990), developed a six-step model for individualizing instruction that involves learners throughout the process.

Many traditional teaching and training situations limit opportunities for such personal involvement. Control over content or process remains in the hands of experts, designers, or teachers who depend primarily on didactic or teacher-directed approaches. In essence, they create barriers to learners assuming personal ownership and thereby foster resistance to self-direction in learning.

Many of these educators may not be familiar with the self-directed learning research and knowledge described above. Some have never taken the opportunity to create a personal statement of philosophy that might help them reevaluate or even reconcile the way they teach or train in relation to what they do know about adults as learners (Hiemstra, 1988). Others follow the instructional patterns to which they were exposed as learners. Still others believe they must adhere to the dictates of an organization's policies regarding instructional procedures and approaches.

In my efforts to help teachers or trainers become more aware of the value of learners taking more responsibility and of ways to empower learners to do so, I often hear comments like the following as reasons why they cannot move to self-directed or individualized instruction: "My content requires that I teach in a very structured, linear approach." "There are state licensure requirements for my students and I must ensure that they obtain a certain level of competency over the content areas." "Your approach might work for some learners, but my trainees do not have the skills to make decisions about their learning activities." Brockett and I (1991) refer to this as the all-or-nothing myth.

At face value, such comments appear to have validity for certain instructors, organizations, or circumstances. However, I contend that what is in force here is the inertia that comes from hours and hours of teaching or learning in a fairly teacher-directed approach. To make changes and overcome such inertia takes hard work at times. In addition, such changes usually will not happen overnight.

One of my responses to this apparent disparity between what self-direction in learning research has demonstrated and much of current teaching or training practice, and to comments like those described above, has been development of the individualized instructional process described above (Hiemstra and Sisco, 1990). In this process we suggest that there are various ways learners can take responsibility for their own learning without leading to anarchy in the learning setting.

For example, learners are involved in assessing their own learning needs early in the process. This provides them with some initial direction for subsequent planning, securing of resources, and focusing their learning efforts. Learners also take considerable responsibility for determining how their learning efforts will be assessed and they are often personally involved in that assessment effort.

In essence, I believe the process of providing opportunities for learners to assume some control is as important as the actual content being covered in a learning effort. In many cases, it may be more important than the content, because the ever-declining half-life of most knowledge greatly enhances the value of helping learners learn how to learn. Understanding how to learn, secure needed resources, and assess learning progress are skills that will successfully carry most learners through a variety of training or instructional situations.

Overcoming Resistance to Promoting Self-Direction

Recently I have begun working on new approaches to helping teachers and trainers of adults think about how their students can assume more personal control over learning efforts. If certain instructors have difficulty accepting all aspects of something like the individualized instructional process described above or other teaching approaches that promote self-direction in learning, they may still find aspects of such processes suitable for incorporation in their instructional approach.

Thus, I have started delineating various ways that learners can assume some control of the learning process. The goal is to provide opportunities for adults to become empowered as self-directed learners even if complete control over the content or the learning process is not possible. I hope that presenting my current ideas in this volume will prompt future research, thinking, dialogue, and refinement.

Therefore, this chapter presents a list of microcomponents or aspects potentially existing in any teaching and learning situation. In essence, each microcomponent provides an opportunity where learners can be encouraged or helped to take increasing personal control. Based on my experience as an instructor for nearly thirty years and my understanding of the self-directed learning knowledge base, I believe most adult learners, if they think they have an opportunity to make some choices, will feel increasingly more empowered with subsequent learning endeavors.

I recognize that giving control to learners can lead to the opening of Pandora's box in terms of such issues as learning focus, quality, and instructors' roles. I have not yet wrestled sufficiently with such issues. Nor am I suggesting that every microcomponent can be dealt with in each learning situation.

In addition, what I am proposing will not necessarily make teaching or training any easier. It has been my experience that the process of giving control to learners or helping them take more control often is hard work for teachers, trainers, and instructional designers. But I am convinced the effort is worthwhile. It helps learners develop approaches and skills of much more value than they get by simply acquiring certain knowledge and then somehow demonstrating that such knowledge has been retained over a certain time period.

Procedure

I used several techniques to extract or develop the microcomponents.

Self-analysis. I analyzed my own teaching, the processes I use, the types of behaviors learners seem to undergo, and the ways adults can be helped to take control of their own learning. This involved studying my teaching evaluations over a couple of semesters, talking with several students about my teaching, and reexamining what I have written about teaching adults in the past several years.

Content analysis of related literature. I carried out an informal content analysis of four books written about teaching adults and five written about self-directed learning to identify some potential microcomponents (Brookfield,

1986; Cross, 1981; Knowles, 1980; Knox, 1986; Long and Associates, 1988, 1989, 1990, 1991; Tough, 1979).

Student assistance. I asked several students in one of my courses to identify what they believed were aspects or parts of the teaching and learning process where learners could assume some control of what took place. Working first individually and then in small groups they identified several components, many of which are incorporated into this chapter.

Initial drafting of ideas. I synthesized the information gathered to this point and developed an initial list of microcomponents. In this process I sought discrete items, clarified the wording, and developed them into a sequential framework.

Collegial assistance. Once I had assembled the first draft of microcomponents I asked two colleagues knowledgeable about individualized instruction and self-directed learning to critique my initial work. They then offered various improvement suggestions, ideas about additional components, and notions about how to portray the set of microcomponents.

Public presentation and feedback. I presented the material at a public session of the Seventh International Symposium on Adult Self-Directed Learning at West Palm Beach, Florida, in 1993. I received various refinement suggestions and ideas from several participants.

Since then, I have continued to refine the list as I obtained new ideas and understandings about teaching and learning. The result thus far is a list of seventy-eight microcomponents pertaining to the teaching and learning process where learners can assume some control. They are grouped under the following headings: Assessing Needs; Setting Goals; Specifying Learning Content; Pacing the Learning; Choosing Instructional Methods, Techniques, and Devices; Controlling the Learning Environment; Promoting Introspection, Reflection, and Critical Thinking; Instructor's and Trainer's Roles; and Evaluating the Learning.

Exhibit 10.1 contains the microcomponents displayed as a checklist that interested teachers can use to determine how they could give learners more control.

I have begun the process of delineating ways learners can take increasing responsibility for various microcomponents. For example, it may be impossible for an interested trainer to allow trainees to specify the learning or instructional objectives (2.1) because such objectives are preset by the organization. However, the trainee could use a learning contract (2.4) to make individual choices on how to achieve the objectives, choices that would build on certain preferences for what to study, the kind of products to develop, or the way mastery will be evaluated.

As an another example, an adult education teacher might believe that the content to be covered must be sequenced in a particular manner (3.2) to ensure that subsequent learning is based on needed precursor knowledge. The learner, though, could make various choices related to the pace of the learning. For instance, choices could be made that teacher presentations were made

Exhibit 10.1. Aspects of the Learning Process
Over Which Learners Can Assume Some Control

1. Assessing Needs
    _____ 1.1 Choosing among various individualized techniques
    _____ 1.2 Deciding whether to use group techniques
    _____ 1.3 Choosing how needs information is reported
    _____ 1.4 Choosing how needs information is used
2. Setting Goals
    _____ 2.1 Deciding on specific learning objectives
    _____ 2.2 Choosing the nature of any learning experience
        _____ 2.2.1 Deciding between competency or mastery learning and pleasure or interest learning
        _____ 2.2.2 Deciding on the types of questions to be asked and answered during learning efforts
        _____ 2.2.3 Choosing the emphases to be placed on use and application of the acquired knowledge or skill
    _____ 2.3 Deciding whether to change objectives during the learning experience
    _____ 2.4 Deciding whether to use learning contracts
        _____ 2.4.1 Choosing among various learning options
        _____ 2.4.2 Choosing how to achieve learning objectives
3. Specifying Learning Content
    _____ 3.1 Choosing among varied levels of difficulty
    _____ 3.2 Choosing a sequence for the introduction of learning material
    _____ 3.3 Choosing the types of knowledge (psychomotor, cognition, affective) to be acquired
    _____ 3.4 Deciding on emphasizing the acquisition of theory versus practice or application activities
    _____ 3.5 Deciding on a level of competency to be acquired
    _____ 3.6 Deciding on actual content areas to be learned
        _____ 3.6.1 Deciding on financial or other costs involved in a learning effort
        _____ 3.6.2 Deciding on the help, resources, or experiences required for the content
    _____ 3.7 Choosing the learning content priorities
    _____ 3.8 Deciding on the major planning type, such as self, a group or its leader, an expert, or a nonhuman resource
4. Pacing the Learning
    _____ 4.1 Choosing the amount of time to be devoted to teacher presentations
    _____ 4.2 Choosing the amount of time to be spent on teacher-to-learner interactions
    _____ 4.3 Choosing the amount of time to be spent on learner-to-learner interactions
    _____ 4.4 Choosing the amount of time to be spent on individualized learning activities
    _____ 4.5 Choosing the pace of movement through learning experiences
    _____ 4.6 Deciding when to complete parts or all of the activities
5. Selecting the Instructional Methods, Techniques, and Devices
    _____ 5.1 Deciding among options for technological support and instructional
    _____   devices
    _____ 5.2 Deciding on the instructional method or technique to be used
    _____ 5.3 Choosing the type of learning resources to be used
    _____ 5.4 Choosing the appropriate learning modality (sight, sound, touch, and so on)
    _____ 5.5 Deciding among opportunities for learner-to-learner, learner-to-teacher, small group, or large group discussion
6. Controlling the Learning Environment
    _____ 6.1 Deciding how to manipulate various physical or environmental features
    _____ 6.2 Deciding how to deal with emotional or psychological impediments
    _____ 6.3 Choosing how to confront social and cultural barriers

_____ 6.4 Deciding how to match personal learning style preferences with informational presentations

7. Promoting Introspection, Reflection, and Critical Thinking
_____ 7.1 Choosing how to interpret theory
_____ 7.2 Deciding on means for reporting or recording critical reflections
_____ 7.3 Deciding whether to use reflective-practitioner techniques
_____ 7.4 Deciding whether to undertake decision-making, problem-solving, and policy formulation activities
_____ 7.5 Choosing how to clarify newly acquired ideas
_____ 7.6 Choosing how to apply newly acquired information

8. Instructor's or Trainer's Role
_____ 8.1 Deciding on the role or nature of any didactic (lecturing) presentations
_____ 8.2 Deciding on the role or nature of any socratic (questioning) techniques to be used
_____ 8.3 Deciding on the role or nature of any facilitative procedures used to guide the learning process

9. Evaluating the Learning
_____ 9.1 Choosing the use and type of any testing
      _____ 9.1.1 Choosing the nature and use of any reviewing activities
      _____ 9.1.2 Choosing the nature and use of any practice testing activities
      _____ 9.1.3 Choosing the nature and use of any retesting activities
      _____ 9.1.4 Choosing how tests will be used in any required grading
      _____ 9.1.5 Deciding on the weight given to any test results
_____ 9.2 Choosing the type of feedback to be used
      _____ 9.2.1 Deciding on the type of feedback provided to learners by an instructor
      _____ 9.2.2 Deciding on the type of learner's feedback provided to the instructor
_____ 9.3 Choosing the means used for validating achievements
_____ 9.4 Choosing the nature of learning outcomes
      _____ 9.4.1 Choosing the type of any final products
            _____ 9.4.1.1 Deciding how evidence of learning is reported or presented
            _____ 9.4.1.2 Deciding how to revise and resubmit final products
            _____ 9.4.1.3 Choosing the nature of any written products
      _____ 9.4.2 Deciding on the weight given to final products
      _____ 9.4.3 Choosing the level of practicality for any learning outcomes
            _____ 9.4.3.1 Deciding how to relate learning to current or future employment
            _____ 9.4.3.2 Choosing how to propose knowledge application ideas
      _____ 9.4.4 Choosing the nature of the benefits from any learning
            _____ 9.4.4.1 Deciding how to propose immediate benefits versus long-term benefits
            _____ 9.4.4.2 Deciding how to seek various types of benefits, such as pleasure, occupational enhancement, or acquisition of new skills
_____ 9.5 Choosing the nature of any follow-up evaluation
      _____ 9.5.1 Choosing how knowledge can be maintained
      _____ 9.5.2 Choosing how concepts are applied
      _____ 9.5.3 Choosing how to review material
      _____ 9.5.4 Choosing how to follow up on new learning
_____ 9.6 Choosing how to exit a learning experience and return later if appropriate
_____ 9.7 Deciding on the type of grading used or completion rewards to be received
_____ 9.8 Choosing the nature of any evaluation of instructor and learning experience
_____ 9.9 Choosing the type of learning contract validation

only during the first half of any class session (4.1) and the latter half devoted to small group work (4.3) or individual study (4.4).

It is my expectation that the microcomponent framework, when it is better understood and refined, will help many learners and teachers or trainers overcome some of their resistance to self-direction in learning. However, this is work in progress and more effort on delineating the components and how they can be used by learners is required. Your feedback, ideas, critique, and comments are welcome.

References

Brockett, R. G., and Hiemstra, R. *Self-Direction in Adult Learning: Perspectives on Theory, Research, and Practice.* New York: Routledge & Kegan Paul, 1991.

Brookfield, S. D. *Understanding and Facilitating Adult Learning: A Comprehensive Analysis of Principles and Effective Practices.* San Francisco: Jossey-Bass, 1986.

Candy, P. C. *Self-Direction for Lifelong Learning: A Comprehensive Guide to Theory and Practice.* San Francisco: Jossey-Bass, 1991.

Cross, K. P. *Adults as Learners: Increasing Participation and Facilitating Learning.* San Francisco: Jossey-Bass, 1981.

Hiemstra, R. "Translating Personal Values and Philosophy into Practical Action." In R. G. Brockett (ed.), *Ethical Issues in Adult Education.* New York: Teachers College Press, 1988.

Hiemstra, R. "Individualizing the Instructional Process: What We Have Learned from Two Decades of Research on Self-Direction in Learning." In H. B. Long and Associates, *Self-Directed Learning: Application and Research.* Norman: Oklahoma Research Center for Continuing Professional and Higher Education, University of Oklahoma, 1992.

Hiemstra, R., and Sisco, B. *Individualizing Instruction: Making Learning Personal, Empowering, and Successful.* San Francisco: Jossey-Bass, 1990.

Knowles, M. S. *The Modern Practice of Adult Education: From Pedagogy to Andragogy.* (Revised ed.) New York: Cambridge, 1980.

Knowles, M. S. *The Adult Learner: A Neglected Species.* (3rd ed.) Houston: Gulf, 1984.

Knox, A. B. *Helping Adults Learn: A Guide to Planning, Implementing, and Conducting Programs.* San Francisco: Jossey-Bass, 1986.

Long, H. B., and Associates. *Self-Directed Learning: Application and Theory.* Athens: Lifelong Learning Research/Publication Project, Department of Adult Education, University of Georgia, 1988.

Long, H. B., and Associates. *Self-Directed Learning: Emerging Theory and Practice.* Norman: Oklahoma Research Center for Continuing Professional and Higher Education, University of Oklahoma, 1989.

Long, H. B., and Associates. *Advances in Research and Practice in Self-Directed Learning.* Norman: Oklahoma Research Center for Continuing Professional and Higher Education, University of Oklahoma, 1990.

Long, H. B., and Associates. *Self-Directed Learning: Consensus and Conflict.* Norman: Oklahoma Research Center for Continuing Professional and Higher Education, University of Oklahoma, 1991.

Tough, A. M. *The Adult's Learning Projects.* (2nd ed.) Austin, Tex.: Learning Concepts, 1979.

ROGER HIEMSTRA is professor of instructional design and adult learning at Syracuse University. He has carried out scholarship related to self-direction in learning for twenty years.

It is possible to overcome sources of resistance to self-direction in learning.

Resistance to Self-Direction in Learning Can Be Overcome

Roger Hiemstra, Ralph G. Brockett

The strategies, applications, and illustrations portrayed in this volume represent the kinds of efforts educators and trainers of adults are making to foster self-direction in learning. Resistance to self-direction is often very real, and it can permeate the experiences of learners, instructors, and institutions. But the examples contained in this volume can provide a sense of optimism and demonstrate that self-direction is possible in virtually any teaching-learning setting. Indeed, the "discovery" of empowerment and the perceived value in turning greater control of the learning process over to the learners is most encouraging. As a way of bringing this volume to closure, we would like to highlight three themes that run through the previous chapters. In addition, we will summarize some of the major strategies for overcoming resistance highlighted in this volume.

Interface Among Learner, Teacher, and Institutional Resistance

One of the most pervasive themes found throughout this volume is that resistance can emanate from learners, from facilitators, and from institutional policies, practices, and attitudes. This distinction is introduced by Long in Chapter Two. Each chapter in this volume looks at resistance from one or more of these vantage points. What is especially important is the way these sources of resistance can interface. For example, institutional policies that resist opportunities for self-direction can be adopted uncritically by instructors. In turn, learners who have never been encouraged to take responsibility for their own learning can remain unaware of the power they possess as learners.

The "All-or-Nothing" Myth

A second theme that permeates the chapters of this volume can be tied directly to the first myth presented by Brockett in Chapter One. The idea that self-direction is an "all-or-nothing" phenomenon places virtually insurmountable barriers to the successful implementation of self-direction in learning strategies because it implies that one must essentially abandon previous ways of working with learners in order to implement self-direction. This is simply not so. The chapters by Jones, Confessore and Confessore, Guglielmino and Guglielmino, Blackwood, and Phelan present scenarios where self-direction can be successfully implemented in many but not all elements of the teaching-learning transaction. The microcomponents presented by Hiemstra in Chapter Ten offer a practical approach for implementing elements of self-direction in virtually any kind of setting.

Overcoming Resistance to Mandatory Continuing Education

The efficacy of mandatory continuing education (MCE) is beyond the scope of this volume. However, MCE is a reality in many organizations and professional fields. One of the criticisms leveled against MCE is that learners who enter such efforts do so with some degree of hostility or resentment at being required to participate in a program. By actively promoting self-direction in such settings, it may be possible to help learners feel some ownership for the program. In this way, self-direction might be helpful in breaking down resistance to participation. While this idea has some potentially important implications, it is also important to remember that this does not resolve questions about the value, appropriateness, or desirability of MCE. In fact, one could argue that self-direction can be used to sell MCE to resistant learners. This is not the position we are advocating, for we believe that there are important ethical questions here regarding the manipulation of learners. But we do recognize that MCE is a reality in many situations and that educators who are charged with developing and delivering such programs have a responsibility to serve learners to the best of their ability. Self-direction holds promise for making this happen.

Some Strategies for Overcoming Resistance

In the previous chapters, each author has presented an array of strategies that learners, teachers, and institutions can use to break down resistance to self-direction. This section highlights some of these approaches.

Learners. For learners, there are at least two factors that can be linked with resistance: self-concept and self-awareness. Many adults enter a teaching-learning transaction with low confidence and poor self-concept, making it difficult to take a high degree of personal responsibility for learning. Other learners, perhaps because of previous experiences with education, are simply not aware of the power they possess as learners and thus make the assumption that a highly teacher-directed approach is the way education should happen. Some of the strategies featured in previous chapters to address this concern include self-reflection, peer reflection and judgments, interviewing techniques that allow individuals to learn from one another, generating lists of possible learning resources, portfolio review and assessment, journal writing, proactive reading, discussions and sharing information with colleagues and peers, learning contracts, and obtaining feedback from many different sources.

Teachers. It is easy to understand why some teachers are reluctant to promote self-direction. Those teachers who hold a more traditional teaching philosophy may see self-direction as a threat to their authority. When learners are viewed as partners in the teaching-learning transaction, they are in a position to suggest content and process different from what has been tried and true to the traditional instructor. Yet the research and practice literature, and indeed, the chapters in this volume, support the idea that the most successful adult learning will take place when learners have an increasing degree of control over and personal investment in the teaching-learning transaction. Strategies that can help to overcome instructor resistance to self-direction include the following:

Teach learners how to be self-reflective
Develop recognition of and rewards for self-directed learning
Provide guidelines for organizing and conducting self-directed learning
    projects
Help learners develop skill in using technology
Use technology for advisement and learner feedback
Help learners learn how to investigate options, opportunities, and resources
Help learners learn how to match individual strengths with interests
Help learners develop education plans
Help learners develop good technical learning skills
Help learners feel comfortable with new content
Help learners enhance their sense of personal learning competence
Help learners develop confidence and skill in taking control of elements of the
    teaching-learning transaction (for example, needs assessment, goal setting,
    selection of content and process, and self-evaluation)
Help learners create and control effective learning environments.

Institutions. Institutional change is often difficult and, when it does happen, is very slow. Yet institutions often present some of the most formidable barriers to self-direction. Those who have responsibility for developing institutional policies need to be willing to think about new and different ways of viewing organizations. An example that quickly comes to mind is Senge's notion of the "learning organization" (1991), which places high value in the human resources of the organization.

A Closing Comment

Self-direction in learning has long ago passed the stage of being a trend or a fad. It is a very real way to think about adult learning and it is here to stay. Elsewhere, we have discussed possible directions for the future of theory, research, and practice related to self-direction (Brockett and Hiemstra, 1991). At the top of those directions, we would encourage future educators to look closely at the issue of resistance. How might theories of resistance contribute to better understanding the full potential of self-direction? How might adult and continuing educators systematically study this area of self-direction? What current and future practices in adult and continuing education and training can help to better understand and overcome resistance to self-direction? If this volume has challenged readers to think about new questions or about old questions from a new angle, then it has served its purpose.

References

Brockett, R. G., and Hiemstra, R. *Self-Direction in Adult Learning: Perspectives on Theory, Research, and Practice.* New York: Routledge, 1991.

Senge, P. M. *The Fifth Discipline: The Art and Practice of the Learning Organization.* New York: Doubleday, 1991.

ROGER HIEMSTRA *is professor of instructional design and adult learning at Syracuse University. He has carried out scholarship related to self-direction in learning for twenty years.*

RALPH G. BROCKETT *is associate professor of adult education in the Leadership Studies Unit, University of Tennessee, Knoxville. He has been involved with self-direction in learning scholarship for fifteen years and is editor-in-chief of* New Directions for Adult and Continuing Education.

INDEX

ORDERING INFORMATION

NEW DIRECTIONS FOR ADULT AND CONTINUING EDUCATION is a series of paperback books that explores issues of common interest to instructors, administrators, counselors, and policy makers in a broad range of adult and continuing education settings—such as colleges and universities, extension programs, businesses, the military, prisons, libraries, and museums. Books in the series are published quarterly in Spring, Summer, Fall, and Winter and are available for purchase by subscription and individually.

SUBSCRIPTIONS for 1994 cost $47.00 for individuals (a savings of 30 percent over single-copy prices) and $62.00 for institutions, agencies, and libraries. Please do not send institutional checks for personal subscriptions. Standing orders are accepted.

SINGLE COPIES cost $16.95 when payment accompanies order. (California, New Jersey, New York, and Washington, D.C., residents please include appropriate sales tax.) Billed orders will be charged postage and handling.

DISCOUNTS FOR QUANTITY ORDERS are available. Please write to the address below for information.

ALL ORDERS must include either the name of an individual or an official purchase order number. Please submit your order as follows:
    Subscriptions: specify series and year subscription is to begin
    Single copies: include individual title code (such as ACE 59)

MAIL ALL ORDERS TO:
    Jossey-Bass Publishers
    350 Sansome Street
    San Francisco, California 94104-1342

FOR SUBSCRIPTION SALES OUTSIDE OF THE UNITED STATES, contact any international subscription agency or Jossey-Bass directly.